A1 03

The Civilized Market

*Corporations, Conviction and the Real
Business of Capitalism*

Ivan Alexander

CAPSTONE

First published 1997 by
Capstone Publishing Limited
Oxford Centre for Innovation
Mill Street
Oxford OX2 0JX
United Kingdom

British Library Cataloguing in Publication Data
A CIP catalogue record for this book is available from the
British Library

ISBN 1-900961-12-1

Typeset in 11/15 pt Palatino by
DP Photosetting, Aylesbury, Bucks
Printed and bound in Great Britain by
T.J. International Ltd, Padstow, Cornwall

This book is printed on acid-free paper

Contents

That's a brilliant idea. But how could it possibly work in my organization?

How often do you think as you read a business book that if only you could ask the author a simple question you could transform your organization?

Capstone is creating a unique partnership between authors and readers, delivering for the first time in business book publishing a genuine after-sales service for book buyers. Simply visit Capstone's home page on **http://www.book-shop.co.uk/capstone/** to leave your question (with details of date and place of purchase of a copy of *The Civilized Market* and Ivan Alexander will try to answer it.

Capstone authors travel and consult extensively so we do not promise 24-hour turnaround. But that one question answered might just jump start your company and your career.

Capstone is more than a publisher. It is an electronic clearing house for pioneering business thinking, putting the creators of new business ideas in touch with the people who use them.

Acknowledgements

Thanks go to Porter Henry, whose long experience and quick understanding are unmatchable on either side of the Atlantic. To Ben Hooberman, for wise advice as always. To Ronnie Lessem, indefatigable examiner of the business mind, for his critical encouragement. To Dick Taverne, classicist, man of law, political affairs and business, whose incisive reading of an early draft was of great value to me. To Dr Richard Burton for good steersmanship, robust good sense and friendship. Profound thanks go to Richard Koch, my able editor, whose many cogent suggestions transformed jottings into a book.

Introduction

" The dollar is innocent. "
Henry David Thoreau, *Civil Disobedience*

The business system – capitalism – envelops our lives, and we have become used to it. It has been startlingly successful in the second half of this century in the West and is now enriching Asia. However obscured this fact may be by arguments, dissatisfactions, recessions and sometimes major failures, business has delivered higher living standards to millions. By so doing it has added not just to the wealth but to the self-esteem of many.

By intent or consequence, the "materialism" of productive corporations has also brought non-material gains – easier and more varied lives. The sustenance (though not the essence) of democracy is another of the gains.

It has condensed space: an acre of factories, banks, shops, malls and office towers yields more than large tracts of fields, farms and forests – not by extension but by intensification.

It is by now evident that the business system will not soon be superseded by radically different economic orchestrations. It will continue to be the envelope of life, but it will not itself be the content of the envelope. Why? Because the capitalist mechanism is a procedure but not, like democracy, a value system.

Capitalism and business were scarcely the products of prior consensus. They were, on the contrary, always the products of passionate contentions, of grudging reconciliations, or, if these were not possible, of acceptable rules of engagement.

Capitalism is a consequence of buffered opposites: management *versus* labour or employees; owners, shareholders or community *versus* management; corporation *versus* corporation; large corporations *versus* small businesses; rule-making corporations *versus* rule-making government; consumers' interests *versus* producers' interests; high returns for the shareholder *versus* low prices for the consumer; exploitation of resources *versus* conservation; cost *versus* social cost; an Ethos of Success *versus* an Ethos of Conviction; protectionism *versus* free trade; national cultures *versus* the transnational rationale of trade and money; monopoly or oligopoly *versus* competition; the need for efficiency *versus* the need for humanity; humanism *versus* humanitarianism; the fairness of equality *versus* the spurs of inequality; tough rationality *versus* compromise.

Added to these is the reality that the administration of individual wealth has now acquired many of the characteristics of corporate administration. Add also that the concepts on which the business system is based – ideas which are the subjects of this book – owe more to force followed by reasonable compromise than to coherence imposed by reason and by logic. These conflicts and contradictions will be encountered and reviewed.

So the business system is not, historically or practically, a product of coherent theories. Vigor and unceasing thrust, but also tolerance and compromise, made it. They continue to make it possible. Business is not an island of self-contained sufficiency. It has always been a permitted mechanism with economic functions and a measure of social utility.

Yet it has not defined its own social locus in society or in the fellowship of nations. Business, even humane business, has no explicit humanitarian role. That role has been assumed by the welfare provisions of the modern state. Though business is a natural carrier of humanism and has a humanistic role, it has not assumed it. Dualism persists: business is still seen as a strange and sometimes alien incubus, with separate ways, mentality and mind from the rest of society. It is not understood, not loved, not even liked.

This separateness of the world of business from society-at-large cannot comfortably continue in a world of foreseeable, ineluctable and increasing closeness and density. This book is about the becoming and foundations of the business system and suggests a more acceptable coherence. It advocates a civilized intent by corporations and their managements.

1

Capitalism and the Horn of Plenty

" Capitalism is an economic-cultural system, organized economically around the institution of property and the production of commodities and based culturally in the fact that exchange relations, that of buying and selling, have permeated most of society. "

" [Joseph A.] Schumpeter once remarked that stationary feudalism was an historical entity, stationary socialism an historical possibility, but stationary capitalism an historical contradiction in terms. "

Daniel Bell, *The Cultural Contradictions of Capitalism,*
1976, pp. 14 and 240.

" Social and political conflict is not now, and in the future
will not be, between capital and labor; it will be between
the comfortably endowed and the [] deprived. **"**
John Kenneth Galbraith,
A Journey through Economic Time, 1994.

*"*THE DISEASE *which sooner or later reaches the heart and brain of a
nation and destroys it, is individualism, that individualism which
recognizes competition between individuals or nations for individual
possessions." Lenin? Stalin? It was said not by Lenin or Stalin but by
King Gillette, the millionaire inventor of the safety razor, in 1910. At
that time, too, the first Henry Ford would not have disagreed substantially with King Gillette.*

*Was it Lenin or Marx who said that it was wrong that a man could
use his property as he pleased, take any number of men into his employ,
and set them to do "whatever work seemed good to him." Not Lenin or
Marx, but Walter Rathenau, a rich and powerful early-20th century
leader of German industry.*

*This chapter is about another capitalism and another epoch, still in
this century but long ago.*

Capitalism and the Horn of Plenty

Unpredicted Triumphs of Capitalism

Six things mark the industrialized world of the second half of this century: immense economic success after many pre-War failures; heightened standards concerning the condition of man both at home and abroad; a global reach; operability in differing cultures; a talent for metamorphosis and transformation; and, still, limited predictability.

In the second half of this century, open-minded democracy, in tandem with capitalism and business, advanced so spectacularly in the West, in Japan and some South-East Asian countries, that what it may suffer stems more from achievement than deficiency.

There were antecedents and anticipations of much that makes it new. The fading of communism's once looming significance is new. The Soviet Union and its tributaries and dependencies forgot Marx's own "principle of temporality" (in *The Poverty of Philosophy*) which states that "ideas and categories are not more eternal than the relations which they express. They are historical and transitory products." Instead, communism monumentalized its system; but what it forged was a handcuffed simulation of eternity.

Communism's lapse was anticipated by the Russian liberal Alexander Herzen in about 1850. Nearly a century and a half ago he said that socialism, then newly born, would develop in all its phases until it reached its own extremes and absurdities. "Then there will again burst forth from the titanic breast of the revolting minority a cry of denial. Once more the moral battle will be joined in which socialism will occupy the place of today's conservatism, and will be defeated by the coming revolution as yet invisible to us."[1] That is what happened.

Again, in 1941, just before Germany attacked the Soviet Union, and about fifty years before its dissolution, the American political philosopher James Burnham guessed that the communist regime might not long continue. In spite of the demonstrated sources of strength in Russia, he said, there were even greater weaknesses. The backwardness of its industry was to be measured not merely in terms of the physical equipment, which was none too good, but equally in terms of the relative scarcity of competent workers and technicians. All these factors would finally give openings to an unusually low grade of careerist in the new state apparatus. He thought that the graft, corruption, and downright stupidity of bureaucracy were unusually widespread in Russia. These weaknesses, he concluded, would be enough to suggest that internal convulsions would be possible.[2] That, too, is what happened.

A Century of Moral Innovations

This century put forth a major moral innovation. While personal charity is very old, beneficence between nations is entirely new. Even though colonialism was already dying, the principle of international aid would anyway have given it the *coup de grâce*, because the idea of colonies will not mix with the idea of international aid. By fateful synchrony, this new regard between nations coincided with the internationalization and transnationalization of business.

The Marshall Plan changed many aspects of the 20th-century world. Yet one humane precursor to it is almost unre-membered:[3] starvation stalked the new Soviet Union in 1921. In July of that year, Herbert Hoover, an anti-communist, then commerce secretary under President Harding, received a per-sonal plea from the Russian writer Maxim Gorky. Surprisingly, he reacted immediately. Russian "cities were filled with mobs crying for food. In Petrograd alone, as many as 100,000 were dying of hunger each month. Then, as now, Russia possessed ample food resources. Then, as now, an incompetent bureau-cratic administration was failing to deliver food where needed. A stupendous famine, centered in the Ukraine and the Volga Valley, gripped the new society. It was caused partly by freaks of weather, but was mainly due to a halt in agricultural production while the Soviets were communizing peasants. Without inter-national help, Lenin wrote then, 'the government will perish'."

" 'At home [in the USA] we were spending unprecedented sums,' Mr Hoover recalled. 'We were undergoing unprece-dented taxation. We were faced with unemployment and all the problems of demobilization of a country regimented to war. Our peopled clamored ... to stop the expense.' Still, the huge US relief effort continued. By the spring of 1922, 18 million Russians were being fed." A staff of about 200 Americans with relief experience had been assembled. At its peak, about 600 Amer-icans were involved. They, in turn, supervised local Soviet workers employed by the US agency that oversaw the movement of supplies from seaports by rail to distribution points throughout the country. Eventually, the relief effort was operating through a distribution network of 18,000 stations. It provided 700 million tons of food, plus a vast store of medicines and commodities. Those supplies fed and nursed 18 million Russians over a three-year period, saving 10 million to 20 million lives.

Afterwards, Maxim Gorky wrote Mr. Hoover: "In all the history of human suffering I know of ... no accomplishment which in terms of magnitude and generosity can be compared to the relief that you have actually accomplished ... Your help will be inscribed in history as a unique, gigantic accomplishment worthy of the greatest glory and will long remain in the memory of millions of Russians ... whom you have saved from death." Stalin saw to it that it did not remain in the memory of the millions of Russians who were saved from death.

Still in Russia, from the early thirties, comes a surprising economic precedent for the European Currency Unit, provisionally called the "euro," as its proposed single currency. The euro is neither mark nor franc, nor lira, florin or pound sterling, but (at least initially) a weighted basket of all these units, together with several others. In the thirties the Chinese Eastern Railway was under joint Soviet–Chinese ownership, but under Soviet management. This independent-minded management, however, trusted none of the local currencies. It invented its own, which it called the "gold ruble." It was neither gold nor a ruble, but an average of several respectable currencies, such as the US dollar, the pound sterling, the Swiss franc, and a few others."[4]

But the earliest (1758) and most relevant anticipation is David Hume's. Hume asked what would happen to "the comparative advantage of nations" when less advanced societies with lower wages learnt to imitate the "mechanic arts" of the first-comers and front-runners. With astonishing prescience Hume asked this question well before the first wave of industrialization swept across British and other shores. According to W.W. Rostow, "Hume's answer, in response to the mercantilist instinct to throttle the latecomers in the cradle, was that the front-runners could enjoy the advantages of expanded two-way trade if [they] maintained an open trading system; but to sustain the inevitably intensified competition, [they] would have to remain, in Hume's words, 'industrious and civilized'."[5]

"The old order changeth, yielding place to new"

One of this century's major innovations was the modern character of capitalism.

In the half-century before World War II, the values and views of the political economy and business, as seen by capitalists as well as by academic observers, were quite unlike our present views. *What was their capitalism is no longer our capitalism.*

Their outlook was defined by the miracle of mass-production. To them, mass-production – or "factory system," "machine system," "productionism," "productivism" – was the new and marvellous revelation that a poor world's needs could be met by the industrial promise of abundance – and that, consequently, mass-production was the handmaiden of humanity.

And yet we would not trade their capitalism for ours because, as we shall see, some of them recommended severe Platonic guardianship too like the fascism and Soviet communism to which it led.

The first academic witness is Thorstein Veblen (1857–1929). The phrases he coined, "conspicuous consumption" and "conspicuous waste," are better remembered than he is. Our reasons for remembering them are of even greater force now than they were in his day. What was then conspicuous has become menacing now.

Veblen was born of Norwegian stock on a Wisconsin farm. All his life he spoke English with a Norwegian lilt. Veblen remained, so one of his friendly critics said, a "visitor from another world." For much of his life his views were unaccepted – because he was a "visitor," because of a failed marriage, and because of other trespasses on prevailing manners and *mores*. He attained fame in later life, but alienation from existing society is the thread that runs through his two most important critiques of capitalism, *The Theory of the Leisure Class* (1899) and *The Theory of Business Enterprise* (1904).

The "industrial" or "machine system," he said, demands discipline, social obedience and efficiency. This was not reconcilable with the age-old barbarism of financial manipulation. An "inhibition of the machine system would push business enterprise to the wall; whereas with a free growth of the machine system, business principles would presently fall into abeyance."[6] Whether you stop or go on, the road, he said, is ending.

The "machine system" was the defining concept of Veblen's day. It was also an underlying concept for another astute observer, Graham Wallas, in 1914. Wallas (1858–1932), Veblen's British contemporary, was, unlike him, a hopeful and benevolently mild socialist. But like him, he was a skeptic who wrote on *Human Nature in Politics* (1908) and on *The Great Society* (1914). He was conscious of the influence of the machine system on civilization, and felt that no satisfactory organization of community on a vast scale was possible. Since "the instinct of accumulation has no clearly defined limits," we must ultimately choose either to live in smaller societies, or pay for the advantages of living in larger societies by constant dissatisfaction with our relations to each other.[7]

Thirty years or so later, in 1942, another observer, Joseph Schumpeter (1883–1950), wrote his influential *Capitalism, Socialism and Democracy*. Schumpeter was Czech-Austrian, decidedly unsocialist, and briefly Austria's minister of finance shortly after World War I. Even as late as World War II, Schumpeter saw ours as a civilization of large and powerful mass-production enterprises, a society of unequal wealth and unprotesting acceptance of involuntary unemployment. This civilization, he said, is destined to die, not as a consequence of its mistakes, but of its virtues, and the success of its process of "creative destruction." Rising incomes, he maintained, undermine the position of entrepreneurs and make them superfluous. Their place is taken by bureaucracy. Not unlike Veblen, he believed that "capitalist activity, being essentially 'rational,' tends to spread rational habits of mind and to destroy those habits of ... subordination that are ... essential for the efficient working of the ... leadership of the producing plant..." A disaffected class of intellectuals arises which resents capitalist inequality. Capitalism undermines the family. But capitalism is itself undermined by inflation. Government can interfere and introduce income equalization, full-employment policies, and policies to ensure stability. These policies themselves undo capitalism. Consequently, socialism will inevitably supersede capitalism.

Schumpeter defined capitalism as a "scheme of values, an attitude to life, a civilization – the civilization of inequality and family fortune."[8] On the whole, this is an overestimate: capitalism is not so much a "scheme of values" as it is a process, a critical procedure, a scheme of pricing and of allocation. Capitalism is part of civilization, but not the main part and not the whole of it. Capitalism is defining, but is not itself defined. We shall return to this.

Now for industrialists, a more interesting sample: Walter Rathenau, Henry Ford I, King Gillette and Ernest Solvay.

Walter Rathenau: "Economics is Fate"

Walter Rathenau's father, Emil (1838–1915) founded the German Edison Company and renamed it AEG (*Allgemeine Elektrizitäts-Gesellschaft*) in 1887. AEG became the German equivalent of the American General Electric Company and the British (but unrelated) General Electric Company. He also laid the foundations, with Werner von Siemens, of the Siemens and the Telefunken corporations. Walter (1867–1922) took over the chairmanship from his father at the turn of the century and made AEG into an enormous corporation. He directed wartime supplies by German industry to the German war effort in World War I (and did so far more effectively than Hitler in World War II with his three agencies which triplicated and split the effort). After the War,

Rathenau became Minister for Reconstruction. In 1922, while now Germany's Foreign Minister, Walter was shot dead by fascists who ignorantly and mistakenly believed that they had killed Walter Rathenau the bad Jewish Cosmopolite, when in fact they had killed Walter Rathenau the good German Patriot. One of those who had been implicated in Rathenau's murder, a writer, Ernst von Salomon, repenting, turned pacifist.

Himself a capitalist of impeccable credentials, Rathenau was both pleased with, and critical of, capitalism. One contemporary witness thought that while he was "seventy-five per cent socialist he was also an aristocrat and a nationalist."[9] Unlike Napoleon, who believed that "fate is politics," Rathenau believed that "economics is fate." Both communism's and capitalism's leaders were agreed that economics and mass-production were keys to a happy future. The intellectual middle classes of the time may have rejected communist theory, but major capitalists like Rathenau only rejected some of its programs.

He wrote this sentence in 1918: "If we spend two to three billions annually on inebriating drinks, sacrifice hundreds of billions on tinsel, show and personal adornment, have tens of thousands of able-bodied salesmen loiter at shop counters in great cities, or have hundreds of thousands of them waste time in railway carriages going forth, year in and year out, to battle their competitors-in-trade, with the result that at the end of the year each company sells a little more or a little less than in the year before – then we squander national savings, misdirect the entire productive process, divert manpower, waste materials, block resources, increase production costs and diminish external competitiveness."[10]

He distrusted petty commerce: "The first small step towards a higher economic morality was that the impersonal [large publicly held corporations] proved to be freer of plots and false advertisement than their ... [small,] closely-held equivalents."

Continuing this theme in another book, he said that executives in major companies "labour for the benefit of times [] when they will long have ceased to be associated with the enterprise." "If offered the choice between having his salary doubled and becoming one of the directors, a leading officer [] will prefer responsibility to wealth." "As a motive force, covetousness has been completely superseded by the sense of responsibility."[11,12] These are hardly observations with which modern observers can unreservedly agree. They reflect views similar to Ford's, and more particularly King Gillette's: large industry is worthy of trust, small companies are untrustworthy legatees of a bazaar mentality.

Another sentence by Rathenau was echoed just a few years later by Henry Ford: "The duty to abolish the more disastrous forms of poverty and want is [] easily fulfilled. The earth is still so abundantly fruitful that there can be ample food, clothing, work and leisure..."[12] This is the "horn-of-plenty" argument. It has little resonance in the late 20th century.

And since we shall turn to the idea of property in Chapter 3, I mention his complaint that in days to come, people will find it difficult to understand how a dead man's will can bind the living. It is wrong that a man can use his property as he pleases, take any number of men into his employ, and set them to do "whatever work seems good to him..." – a curiously anti-establishment sentiment from one of the great industrial entrepreneurs of the 20th century.

Though out of place here (see Chapter 2) I cite his wry words on another of our subjects, the idea of progress: "In everchanging combinations, capitalism, invention, Calvinism, Judaism, luxury, the service of women, are interwoven as alleged evolutionary factors of the course of events. No one seems to notice that in this way one miracle is continually being explained by another..." Rathenau said this in 1916, while running Germany's war economy. His reading was up to date;

unmistakably, the reference here is to the writings of two eminent German sociologists and historians, Max Weber and his
friendly rival Werner Sombart. Weber had published *The
Protestant Ethic and the Spirit of Capitalism* in 1904/5, Sombart *The
Jews and Modern Capitalism* in 1911, and *Luxury and Capitalism* in
1913.

Rathenau believed that consumption was less an individual
than a communal activity; that property and income ought to be
more equal; that monopoly, speculation and inherited wealth
ought to be abolished, and luxury restricted. In the end, it turns
out that Rathenau was a corporate syndicalist whose solutions,
had they been applied, would have been similar to Lenin's "state
capitalism." Rathenau, a capitalist, called his solution the "de-
individualization of ownership," Lenin, a communist, the
"public ownership of the means of production, distribution and
exchange."

Henry Ford: "To be rich is no longer a common ambition"

And now, Henry Ford (1863–1947) writing in the twenties.[13]

"My effort," he says, "is in the direction of simplicity.
People in general have so little and it costs so much to buy even
the barest necessities (let alone that share of the luxuries to which
I think everyone is entitled) because nearly everything that we
make is much more complex than it needs to be. Our clothing,
our food, our household furnishings – all could be much simpler
than they now are and at the same time be better-looking." (A
point also made by Rathenau.) He continues: "We are growing
out of this worship of material possessions. It is no longer a
distinction to be rich. As a matter of fact, to be rich is no longer a
common ambition. People do not care for money as money, as
they once did. Certainly they do not stand in awe of it, nor of him
who possesses it. What we accumulate by way of useless surplus
does us no honor." This is Ford's version of what became known

as the Gospel of Wealth after Andrew Carnegie, the Pittsburgh steel magnate, had said that "the millionaire should be ashamed to die rich."

Ford, too, inclined to industrial syndicalism and to contempt for competition: "Whoever does a thing best ought to be the one to do it." He did not say how best-ness would be judged. Next, profit ought not to be maximized: "Manufacturing is not buying low and selling high. It is the process of buying materials fairly and, with the smallest possible addition of cost, transforming those materials into consumable product and giving it to the consumer."

Eccentrics are the cartoonists of the conventional wisdoms of their times. Ford and Rathenau took the received ideas of their day and applied the logic of the new industrialism to them.

King Gillette: Competition is the Disease

The next witness, however, King C. Gillette (1855–1932), the inventor of the safety razor, reduced them to absurdity. I take him almost last, although he wrote a few years before Ford and Rathenau; and I do this to compare his thesis with theirs. Behind Gillette's outrageous conclusions are many identities of reasoning.

Like Rathenau, Gillette disliked competition. M.L. Severy, Gillette's adjutant until sacked, said – with evidently high regard for synonyms – that "competition is un-Christian, immoral, corruptive, unjust, inequitable, iniquitous, wasteful, brutal, uncertain, chaotic, and inefficient."[14] Three years later, in 1910, Gillette himself wrote that "the disease which sooner or later reaches the heart and brain of a nation and destroys it, is individualism, the individualism which recognizes competition between individuals or nations for individual possessions..." "The real purpose of the machine of industry is to supply the necessities of life." "Those industries which do not contribute to these ends are waste..."

More even than Rathenau, Gillette admired the massive corporation. "Economy, stability, and absence of friction are striking characteristics of Large Corporations." "Graft, as far as the United States Steel Corporation is concerned, is at an end." "Look about you. See what individuals are doing. [Then] look at the United States Steel Corporation, the Railroad Corporation, the Standard Oil Company, the Sugar Trust, the Telephone and Telegraph Monopoly, and the thousands of corporations that are binding together in corporate harmony millions and millions of money, and thousands upon thousands of individuals, and centralizing intelligence and power in a manner unknown in any former history of the world. [They] are there by bringing order out of chaos..." "The Standard Oil Company is an example of a rational governmental industrial system, if you eliminate stockholders, who as such are not necessary to its operation." "The monumental blunder of the century is the restraint put upon centralization by the Sherman [Anti-trust] Act."[15]

One of his more *outré* ideas was that of a "World Corporation." The World Corporation is "destined to combine Education, Industry, and Government throughout the world in one system, bringing all nations and all peoples into one corporate body, possessing one corporate mind ... regardless of nationality, race, creed, color, age, or sex. It recognizes dollars, not individuals." It will be "the great industrial absorber of the world," "the only employer of labor and the only seller of products." It will be "the materialized embodiment of millions of minds, centralized and working in harmony, [and] will be so wonderful and so beautiful in its mechanism that only its realization can bring it within range of our comprehensions."

"The Corporate Mind of the people will control, direct, and manage the whole industrial field of the world." "Under the 'World Corporation' farm labor to the number of five million [in the USA will be] organized into armies, and moved in companies

and detachments under the supervision of skilled agricultural-
ists..."

Gillette was outlandish. His thoughts would have led to an
exaltation of the state as the throne of legitimacy, similar to
Hegel's state; except that in Gillette "the Corporation" wholly
replaces the state. And if we substitute Gillette's fascist "World
Corporation" for Marx's and Lenin's "Dictatorship of the
Proletariat" (as interpreted by Stalin), what difference in effect
remains?

Ernest Solvay and "Productivism"

Ernest Solvay (1838–1922) was a Belgian and a moderate; which
suits the present argument well lest it be thought that the three
previously mentioned exponents were atypical eccentrics. Solvay invented and cartelized a process for producing soda ash in
1863, which he manufactured in many countries and which
brought him great wealth. Yet he was against the inheritance of
wealth. He proposed that money be replaced by an alternative
method of social accounting. He held celebrated scientific
seminars which the best scientists of the day attended: Albert
Einstein, Max Planck, DeBroglie, Sir James Jeans, Lord Ruther-
ford, Madame Curie, and many others.

In a letter he wrote in the eighties of the last century, Ernest
Solvay expressed his conviction that "... the future belongs to
big corporations and common-interest organizations; it is the
price we must pay for an assured future." According to a
chronicler, Solvay held the view that progress would primarily
depend on large-scale production. As a countervailing power to
bigness, Solvay "defended the policy of rapid improvements in
social security. Some supporters of the working class disliked
this because he pleaded their cause without belonging to their
party. He astounded the liberals; and he frightened the
conservatives."[16]

In the first decade of this century he gave his "rationalization of industry and the national economy" the name "productivism." He was not an immodest man, but in an often cited letter he wrote in 1879, said that "I must solve the problems of the universe."

Our four industrialists were exponents of a spirit of capitalism which has largely disappeared. The process which is capitalism, and the critical procedure which it also is, have done their work since then. The old order changed and yielded place to new. The great realities they saw – power, the machine-system, mass-production, "productivism," the possibility of standardized consumption, the abundance of the earth – have either vanished or receded. Their cures were different. Few of them would occur to us today.

Vladimir Ilyich Lenin: Capitalists as "Pacemakers of Socialism"

There is an immense irony of history in all this. Lenin once said that "communism is Soviet power plus the electrification of the whole country." This was shorthand for power applied to mass-production. But the source of the people's wealth was to be the same as Gillette's, Ford's, Rathenau's and Solvay's: the productivity of mass manufacture. The capitalists, as well as Lenin, shared a disdain for ordinary commerce. In the creation of national wealth, too, Lenin's vision and theirs were almost identical. In Lenin's view, the Soviet state could be regarded as "not the successor of capitalism but a parallel alternative."[17] "Can the Soviet state," he asked, "be combined, united with state capitalism? Are they compatible? Of course they are."[18] *There was more kinship of view between Ford and Rathenau, and Lenin, than between either and late 20th century democratic capitalism.* Joseph Schumpeter has observed that "[t]he true pacemakers of socialism were not the intellectuals and agitators who preached it but the Vanderbilts, Carnegies and Rockefellers."

Lenin created a state based on this industrial vision. It was a capitalist vision. Our present economic order left it behind. But this early 20th-century vision of the Horn of Plenty became a principle for the organization of the Soviet state – and it never changed. Quantity remained the ideal; all the other characteristics of a balanced economy – quality, the costing of opportunities, competition, service, efficiency, maintenance, distribution – remained unseen by the single cyclopean eye of raw, titanic output. For over seventy years, the Soviets stuck to it, tried to make it work, and failed.

Historians of political ideas may recognize that belief in the marvels of technology and the superiority of technocrats goes back to Count Henri de Saint Simon (1760–1825), and that the evils of competition were earlier condemned by Charles Fourier (1772–1837). Such historians may also be tempted to conclude that from the late 18th until the second half of this century industrialism rather than capitalism dominated the economic vision of the world. We are in this respect perhaps closer today in outlook to Renaissance Venice, Florence and the Netherlands, and to their ways of trade and their views of money, than to 19th- and early 20th-century Europe, the United States and Soviet Russia.

Industrialization Continues: "Post-industrialism" is Hardly What it Seems

There is a postscript to the above.

The age of industrial mass-production has not ended as either an economic or a philosophical reality. There was, and still is, wealth-making truth in the concept, and there is – in such as the inorganic chemicals and petroleum industries – almost no alternative industrial procedure. But a shift has taken place in another sector: in mass-production services.

The grouping of supply into the two classical 19th-century categories of industry and services no longer holds. Seen by the consumer there still is a difference between a physical product and a service ("services can't be stored"). Seen by the producer, there is hardly any in terms of either management or methods. The age of industrialization continues, but it continues in the industrialization (and partly storability) of services. The industrialization of language, for example – in print, through cables, through the air and space – is now one of the world's great industries. Much of agriculture and horticulture, once considered separate economic sectors, have acquired the characteristics of a services–industrial complex. The Dutch flower industry, for example, has, in science, scale, and brilliant distribution, become a model complex of this kind. About 80 percent of Holland's roses, chrysanthemums and carnations are flown to global destinations within hours of harvesting.

If, therefore, one must classify, one must classify (alas, I have no better term for it) into the categories of industrial-mass-production-plus-industrialized-mass-services on the one hand, and personal (rarely exportable) services on the other – the services of doctors, nurses, corporate lawyers, accountants, artists, conductors, firemen, teachers, policemen, acrobats, and the like.

There is now more capitalization per employee in such industrialized services as banking, airlines or international currency trading than in most traditional manufacturing. It could indeed be said that manufacturing industry has lately been a stepchild of investment flows. Western industries have far too often shunned expensive reequipment debt. Instead of investment in labor-saving machinery, methods and materials, many of them sloughed manual work off to sweaty *maquiladoras* in ill-paid countries. Now, there is little wrong in providing work for striving peoples. Indeed, a great deal is right with it: they will become rich customers one day. What is wrong is that the move to them is often made from inertia, laziness, and fear of the risks of capital investments.

Except by product, and that only sometimes, it is difficult to distinguish industrial mass-production from service mass-production – even within one corporation. The "service" component in General Motors, an industrial corporation, is more than half its turnover. So are software and service components in the computer industry. And thus the age of industrialization continues into the next century: services become part industries and industries become part services.

Germany and Japan have continued to rely on industrial mass-production as the main engine of wealth creation in the national economy. Though their success has been great, it may lessen as they reach the end of the century. Neither Japan nor Germany have been lively enough in what have been considered services so far. In a sense, Germany and Japan are old-fashioned industrial philosophers. They grew rich by conventionally efficient mass-production, became conventionally satisfied by the ways of their banks, insurance companies and distribution systems, and are sated by the life and welfare all these made possible. This does not mean that they will fail. The Japanese, as also the Germans, are cohesive and sensible people. They will adapt to altered circumstances.

The world faces the fact that *completed* new and efficient investment appears to displace people. If this is so, only the investment process itself can bring significant additions to employment (because a surge in new building, and the provision of the tools to fill them, swells work immediately though passingly). But it is doubtful whether there is, beyond this, any *proportionate* link between the general level of investment and the general level of employment in an advanced economy.

The world's volume of manufactured products and mass-production services has not decreased. But fewer people are needed to make and provide them, and real costs have fallen.

Not the cost of manufactured products and major services, but the cost of many personal services has risen disproportionately. The real distinction is not between industry sectors and service sectors, but between such activities as can be industrialized and such as cannot be industrialized.

Yet the argument that for purposes of national wealth it does not matter where investment falls provided it gives the same return, is false. The argument that an economy of services alone is as good as any is also false. This can be true in the short term, but not for long. Clearly, though the efficiency of most personal services can be improved, it cannot be substantially improved. Rail services, restaurants, film-making, hospitals, tourism or postal services may do well by decreasing inputs by perhaps a fifth or so, and yet maintain their outputs. By comparison, as history has shown, industrial efficiency has few upper limits: in a few decades cables have increased their carrying capacity by many powers; the efficiency of, say, refrigerator, washer and car-manufacture has seen many-fold multiplications year by year. In the long run, the external competitive advantage of service-based countries (whose efficiency goes up by a few percent per year, if at all) is low when compared with manufacturing countries (whose annual efficiency can go up by many more). No *major* country can be a kind of Switzerland, making a living from battalions of tourists, not even Switzerland. She has grown richer by making pharmaceuticals, foods and advanced textile machinery efficiently, and by using knowledgeable banks with expensive but thorough computer systems.

It *does* in the end matter whether money is made by currency trading and the shuffling of financial derivatives, or whether it is made by inventive engineering, material and computer sciences, satellites, and complex tools and dies.

Summary

Industrial mass-production was the world-saving horn of plenty at the start of the century. It is no longer seen as such.

Mass-production still exists; in absolute terms it is stronger than ever. Indeed, it is extending to the industrialization of "services," some of which are more highly capitalized than traditional manufacturing. "Post-industrialism" is largely a misnomer.

The world will find answers to the proximate problems of industrial production and major services. Their health is reasonably excellent and their outputs more efficient than ever. But one of their former inputs – people who have lost their jobs – will be quick to disagree with this diagnosis. The world's serious concerns will be the place of business in the modern world, and the markets' future ferments. They will be the subjects of later chapters.

2

Capitalism and Progress

" Those who do not want to insult the creator should be careful not to insult his creation. "
Theodor Haecker, *Journal*, 1939–1944

" In everchanging combinations, capitalism, invention, Calvinism, Judaism, luxury, the service of women, are interwoven as alleged evolutionary factors of the course of events. No one seems to notice that in this way one miracle is continually being explained by another. "
Walther Rathenau, *In Days to Come*, 1916

In a sense, progress is the idea that man is not a pawn in a game but master of his destiny, that time is no enemy, and that there is time enough to seek improvement.

There is an affinity between humanism, the idea of progress and the business outlook. Business, too, thinks that it is not a pawn but master of its game, that there is enough time to seek improvement, that time is not an enemy but a resource. By its own nature, business tries to put certainties into nature's uncertain frame.

On the other hand, even those who believe in progress no longer hold, as once they did, that nature is unexhausted and inexhaustible and that land is limitless. Yet we still cautiously continue to believe that science is an endowment of power, and that we, in Dryden's words, may go upon our globe's last verge and view the ocean leaning on the sky.

Though we are now aware that the riches of the earth are finite, we have discovered other dimensions of opportunity, a new compacted yet fertile space in which business can flourish and expand. Trade, commerce, automation, robotics and informatics, though almost landless and spaceless, offer unbounded opportunities. Computers are the least dimensional machines mankind has yet devised.

Capitalism and Progress

"Nothing that is vast enters into the life of mortals without a curse."

Sophocles, *Antigone*

"We cannot be certain 'to what height the human species may aspire in their advance toward perfection...'. We may therefore safely acquiesce in the pleasing conclusion that every age of the world has increased, and still increases, the real wealth, the happiness, the knowledge, and perhaps the virtue, of the human race."

Edward Gibbon, *Decline and Fall of the Roman Empire*

"Myths are public dreams."

Joseph Campbell

The Idea of Progress

In the early thirties, in *The Idea of Progress*, J.B. Bury remarked that if there were good cause for believing that the earth would be uninhabitable in 2000 or 2100 AD the doctrine of progress would lose its meaning and automatically disappear.[1] And in 1980, Robert Nisbet's *History of the Idea of Progress* sadly concluded that only in the context of a culture in which the core is a deep sense of the sacred are we likely to regain the vital conditions of progress itself and of faith in progress.[2]

Bury may turn out to be right, but we need not let him be right. Nisbet is less likely to be right. The Idea of Progress flowered most abundantly when belief in God's unalterable works was, from approximately the end of the 17th century, gradually succeeded by faith in man's abilities. The image of man as his own great resource began to replace the image of nature as the created miracle.

On the contrary, G.K. Chesterton said, our modern world is in some ways far too good: it "is full of wild and wasted virtues. When a religious scheme is shattered, as Christianity was shattered after the Reformation, it is not merely the vices that are let loose. The vices are, indeed, let loose, and they wander and do damage. But the virtues are let loose also; and the virtues wander more wildly, and the virtues do more terrible damage."[3]

Post-Soviet Russia, for example, is a land of errant virtues. His antagonist, Boris Yeltsin, asked in 1990 why Gorbachev had started climbing a mountain whose summit was not even visible. Yeltsin made an unexpected guess: not because of the economy, but because Gorbachev detested hypocrisy and lies, and because a last effort had to be made to civilize the country after the communist "true realm of freedom" (which would blossom out of the "realm of necessity") had done no such thing.[4]

Gorbachev "detested lies." So did Yeltsin. For a few years there were fewer *official* liars in Russia than anywhere. The West has not seen the abandonment of communism in the former Soviet Union as mainly *moral* progress. Yet it has been an example of ideology swapped for some straightforward moral ideas (which may of course fail. The vices have been let loose also). The idea of the Perfectibility of Man has been abandoned by the Russians, and the use of social instruments to "improve" him by *ukase*, official command, has been discontinued. But a great deal still needs to be done because, while material progress may permeate rapidly, moral progress shuffles forward slowly and uncertainly. The privatization of "Soviet man" means that he will have to seek his own perfectibilities. This has not yet been understood by many Russian citizens. Free enterprise cannot take well in any nation that does not have men and women who, though not rich themselves, have seen wealth-producing mechanisms at work, and have seen them become socially responsible. Russian citizens cannot be blamed. As I write, few wealth-producing mechanisms are at work there, and fewer still are socially responsible.

If a genuine sense of the sacred (Nisbet's) is nowhere to be found, and if the earth (Bury's) becomes less comfortable in the 21st century, are we done with the Idea of Progress? Ask people in business for their assessment of the state of things, and whether this is the last age of the world, and they will tell you that it is not the springtime of the world but not the last age either. They will say that for some of the many who think that the idea of progress is nearly dead, there are others who have eradicated yellow fever and have walked on the moon. They will agree that there are few certainties, that many virtues have to run to courts of law for definition, but, also, that business is no place for gloomy people.

The Progress of the Idea of Progress

"Progress" did not escape the vision of the ancient Greeks. But the times were inauspicious, and the same acuity of mind that let them see the possibilities of progress also made them skeptical of it. Men, they knew, could grow to virtue, but it is doubtful that they would, indefinitely.

The Middle Ages abandoned the seesaw view of history for a linear view – an arrow of time. But these medieval times, the Last Age, St Augustine's "old age of humanity," could not carry the idea of progress. Original Sin and Divine Providence were not compatible with it. In any case, everything was bounded: earth was in the hands of powerful feudal lords. Fixed above the earth lay the unmoving spheres of crystal and the domain of God. In the medieval understanding, a renaissance could, in the literal sense of the word, only be the rebirth of suitably qualified persons into a suitably ordained millennium – at a time not far distant, of God's choosing, and beyond man's. God had arranged the world; the world was not a playground for human rearrangements.

Until the 18th century, physical constraints made unlimited growth impossible and unimaginable. Wind, water, burning wood and animal power were the only forms of energy. Hygiene was rudimentary, transport expensive, land held by incumbents. There was little science and not enough technology.

Few voices before Francis Bacon's spoke of the need for science. One rare exception was Peter Abelard (c. 1079–1142), founder of Paris University, who said that many people are practiced in action but have little scientific understanding. They do not know much about natural causes. "The man of understanding is he who has ability to grasp and ponder hidden causes of things. By hidden causes we mean those from which things originate, and these are to be investigated more by reason than by sensory experiences." His voice went unheard for many centuries.

Such were the constraints before the Industrial Revolution; before the interrogation of nature's "immutable laws" by science; before the realization, sometimes conscious, that Europe was no longer Rome prolonged; before the acceptance of Francis Bacon's view that scientific knowledge has immediate utility; and before created man became creative man – Montesquieu's man, Voltaire's, Comte's, American man, man more causing than caused, hopeful and rational. Edward Gibbon felt certain of progress when he wrote that every age of the world has increased, and still increases, the real wealth, the happiness, the knowledge, and perhaps the virtue, of the human race.

The early Middle Ages had lived in anticipation of the sunset of a world which, they proclaimed, was growing old and awaited its deliverance. Humanism and the Enlightenment dismissed this temporality and, newly hopeful, proclaimed a sunrise. The present age is the only one that we have ever known in which unlimited growth has been a realistic vision. Concepts grew in an unfolding world which took boundlessness for granted: the Inevitability of Progress, *l'Esprit humain*, the Dignity of Man, the Perfectibility of Man, Representative Democracy, the Pursuit of Happiness, Marxism, Socialism, Free Enterprise, Free Trade. Imagination was no longer confined by the finite. Men were now free to be engineers of their own salvation; and as a corollary, men saw their own nature – human weakness and inconstancy – as the only remaining constraint to an eternity of possibilities. And, to paraphrase R.H. Tawney, at the same time as the modern temper took our destinations for granted, it grew enthralled by the hum of the engines.

The meaning of space has shifted. Until recently, the world had had two dimensions: one could grow only so much on an acre of land. Now, space has increased by intensification: one square mile of city or factory generates economic value vastly greater than its acreage. Cities and factories reside in economic space; and there are more measurements of the amplitude of economic space than length and breadth.

The Theory of Games: a Science of Restraint

There was another shift: the meaning of rationality divided in two. One division inclined to a "scientific" rationale for government – to a centralizing philosophy and to socialism, which hoped that it could transform the play by a radical rearrangement of the scenery. To the surprise of many, it did badly –

its adherents having, in Hazlitt's phrase, "lost their way in Utopia, as usual."

The other took a very different direction: the "logic" of self-interest, which sometimes coincided with virtue though there seemed to be no necessary connection. This logic, Adam Smith's logic, modern everyday logic, unsurprisingly assumes that man – individually, corporately, or nationally – properly prefers advantage to disadvantage, greater advantage to lesser advantage, minor disadvantage to major disadvantage. It is perhaps curious that this atomistic approach has proved to be more durable and practical than "scientific" rationality, and that democratic unity can flourish amid great diversity. But rationality is now on the side of jostling for advantage and the Theory of Games.

The theory is abstract and mathematical; but essentially it asks what the outcome might be of a "rational" or "optimal" choice of action by an individual (or group, or company) when faced with equally "rational" and equally "optimizing," but different strategy of other individuals (or groups or companies) – even when all of them obey the same basic rules of the game. The game may be a war; it may be football; or it may be business competition. What is it that is rational? The decision, or its outcome? One of them? Both? Or neither?

This logic of games, Leibniz first said, is "the best representation of human life," of economic behaviour, of competitive behaviour, of profit maximization, of free trade, of the consumer society. It is the logic of the economic system, of free enterprise, business and capitalism, in which independent but interacting agents each pursues his own goal. But while this logic is rational within the terms of the game it is not a logic of giving and conceding reasonableness and charity. Business and the capitalist world earn their living by pugnacious games – games that are fortunately wealth-creating and efficient; but also games that are often pitiless to losers.

Oskar Morgenstern, co-author with John von Neumann of the *Theory of Games and Economic Behaviour*,[5] in 1944, says that in such a world no formal set of rules can be found which is complete: any set will prove to be either incomplete or self-contradictory. Society must adopt the best available set of rules, and make new rules where the old ones fail in particular cases. Being by nature incomplete, every social theory in a free society must be prepared to amend itself: "new games can always be invented" to serve as improved models.[6]

But, they claimed, the hope of finding a uniquely best solution for human affairs is vain and there is no stability in such arrangements. Only a fully centralized, usually dictatorial, society could produce such a scheme that it considered better than any other [the Soviet Union did] and it hoped to be able to enforce [the Soviet Union could not].

Isaiah Berlin, great modern humanist but no game theorist, reinforces this opinion: " 'Immanuel Kant ... once observed that out of the crooked timber of humanity no straight thing was ever made.' And for that reason no *perfect* solution is, not merely in practice but in principle, possible in human affairs, and any determined attempt to produce it is likely to lead to suffering, disillusionment and failure."[7] (The emphasis on "perfect" is mine. No one need despair of adequate solutions.)

Games have rules and there are winners and losers. In some games all win, but there are winners and losers in many games, and only losers in others. And in so far as there are losers, there can be no innate and universal tendency to happiness in economies of games. One must forgo the argument that inevitable progress (or any other kind of progress) will bring inevitable happiness. A balance sheet can, of course, exist in which, by some unfathomable calculus, the sum of all happinesses exceeds the sum of all unhappinesses. But a calculus of general utility cannot console losers. Like the peace of God, it would remain beyond understanding.

At first glance the theory of games is cold and sad. Winning appears to have no purpose beyond the victory. And yet it merits second glances. The "prisoner's dilemma," a scenario which is typical of gaming choices, shows that an optimal solution may be found in tolerant and tacit reciprocity rather than outright business wars. Game theory is down to earth and leaves room for the "least-worst" choices so common in the world of business.

It is our good fortune that not everything in liberal economies is games. However high the degree of economic liberality, games are not a sufficient substitute for fair laws and governance. What the contemporary American writer George Wills calls "ennobling functions" remain. There are gaming choices, and choices outside the game, to be made in politics and commerce – choices between enduring gain and present profit. It is at any rate certain that a successful social order is one in which the recommendation to "enrich yourself" means a great deal more than a fat purse.

In moral conduct, too, there are choices (which are not part of any game) to be made between traditional sanctities, and future benefits which have yet to become holy. Some unresolved dualisms are unsuitable for the 21st century. Take this statement, for example: "Because life is sacred, don't interfere with human heredity," *versus* this statement: "Because life is sacred, interfere to ensure health and adequate resources." Future sanctities will have to be carefully selected.

Progress is no longer, as Fontenelle, Condorcet and others may have believed at the end of the 17th and in the 18th century, the unfolding of human ability and goodness indefinitely, necessarily and certainly. Instead, progress is a duty; progress is conditional; progress is not only development but also maintenance: a list of things that must be done to blunt the shears of Atropos which cut the thread of life.

Progress, Evolution and Social Darwinism

Progress is a form of evolution but not a form of natural evolution. Being hopeful, Darwin himself thought that his theory implied progress. Natural selection, he said, "works solely by and for the good of each being, [and] all corporeal and mental endowments will tend to progress towards perfection."[8] But Darwin's theory does not sustain Darwin's argument.

Nature deals in survival; it is not concerned with perfection. Plants and animals are only as "perfect" as they need to be. Useless vestiges, like the appendix, remain; the urinary system shares organs with the reproductive system. As long as things work adequately, nature does not continue to refine. It operates on the unforgettable principle first enunciated by an anonymous Texas automobile mechanic: "if it ain't broke, don't fix it."

Natural evolution provides no support for those who believe that progress is inevitable. There is no ideal of perfection in nature: rats are as perfect as roses. There is no ideal of beauty in nature: rats are as beautiful as roses.

In nature as in the economics of the firm, equality does not help. Over time, it is the advantage of superior inequality that provides the edge. In nature, inequality happens; in the corporation it is intended. The same goes for equality of opportunity. On the face of it, equality of opportunity is the opposite of equality because it is a license to display advantage over others. Neither business nor Darwinian evolution are egalitarian.

In a sense, man is not a natural species. Civilizations are more artifice than "nature." Unlike nature, societies have courtesies, conventions, rules of conduct, codes of law. Any of these may be either necessary or convenient; but not one of them is "natural." Behind each is a rational recognition of some necessity, even if it is only the rationale of selfish power. A natural species has been defined as a group that cannot normally carry information – in the form of genes – to another species. In human cultures, however, information is constantly carried from one group to other groups. No culture is now isolated from influences radiated by another. Human cultures, including such subsets of them as businesses and corporations, are "complex adaptive systems" which continuously respond to altered circumstances. Acquired wisdoms – and, alas, acquired follies also – are culturally heritable. Cultural evolution, therefore, is often more Lamarckian than Darwinian. (It includes publicly quoted corporate dinosaurs with acquired sluggish habits.)

Nature often errs but never admits its mistakes. In the sense that it makes no judgements when it creates or destroys, nature is never wrong. But civilization, in the words of T.H. Huxley, is "a checking of the cosmic process at every step." Natural evolution, he said, "encourages no millennial expectations." But in human society there are purposes, judgements and apologies.

Natural evolution has no mechanism to oppose change. An individual within a natural species cannot act within his own lifetime and cannot bend immediately when challenged. A species cannot light a fire when cold, or quickly grow a new fur coat. If there is a sudden mismatch between a species and its circumstances, so much the worse for the species. But mankind's history is, to a large extent, the story of struggles to accommodate change or to prevent it.

The individual plays a puny part in nature. The survival of a species does not depend on the saintliness or heroism of a single animal or plant. It does in the history of man; and it does – not saintliness and heroism, but common sense – in every business.

Then, too, democracy is a difficult attempt which nature has not tried.

Punishment by death – nature's sole and certain penalty – is held in check in a civilization. The penalty of death may be judicial or arbitrary; but it is always intentional and deliberate.

In questions of life and death, nature has only the *how*, but civilization wants to know *why*. One has its mechanisms, the other looks for causes and justifications. Cause in history is usually obscure. And so civilization has often had recourse to myth. Myth is used by man as dogs use lamp posts: only partly for illumination.

Progress and Myth: A False and Frozen Explication

Without myth, art would have been impoverished. Few temples would have been built, or sculptures fashioned, or paintings painted, had myths not been their subjects and their motive. Much that is sacred and good in human society would not have bloomed. But much that is sacred but bad in human society would have been omitted.

Myth is substitute causality. The religious philosopher Étienne Gilson suggests that the origin of myth is to be found in the firm decision of classical man not to be left alone in a world without significance, amidst deaf and dumb things.

Much later the views of science and myth diverged. Science does not deny that a future golden age is possible, but cannot discover any in the past. Myth, on the other hand, can accept every possibility: that there was once a golden age which will return; that there was once a golden age which will not return; that there was no golden age but that a golden age is coming or may come; that there never was a golden age and none will ever come; and finally that, anyway, a golden age is not for earth but heaven.

Furthermore, science is troubled when it does not know and does not understand. It teases away at every How but leaves the Why of the universe to philosophers and myth-makers. It accepts temporary truths but refuses temporary lies.

Myth is more facile. It is sometimes hope-bestowing and benign, as, for example, concerning the Resurrection. Sometimes it is vicious, as, for example, concerning Hitler's myth of race.

Sometimes it is passionless, as in Homer's thanatology, according to which the dead in Hades are not punished by eternal torture but by an everlasting recollection of the shame of their lives. Sometimes it is ambivalent, as when some centuries after Homer, Socrates spoke of the dead, who, when ennobled by philosophy, would be moved to the purest regions and share the ether with the gods. We should live, he thought, *as though* this myth were true because it was at least "a belief worth risking."[9] Reminiscent of this was Pascal's Wager in the 17th century, which in effect said: "Bet on faith. If it is true, you may win eternal life; if it is false, you have lost nothing." Sometimes, rarely, myth tells the sober truth, such as that man only became recognizably himself when he acquired a knowledge of good and evil after the Fall.

Some myths contain a grain, or several, of truth. Others were hardly distinguishable from superstition: the Starover sect in Russia, the Old Believers, were said to have refused to use postage stamps on the grounds that these were the "Mark of the Beast." The Russian Orthodox Church disapproved of shaving because beards belonged to the image of God. Quakers refused to raise their hats to each other because they believed that all men are equal. Jehovah's Witnesses refused insurance because it showed no confidence in Divine Providence.

Myths are inconstant and often change their masters. Betrand Russell illustrates this by a "dictionary" which translates Old Testament terms into communist terms: Yahweh equals Dialectical Materialism; the Messiah equals Marx; The Elect equal The Proletariat; The Church equals The Party; The Second Coming equals The Revolution; Hell equals the Eviction of Capitalists; The Millennium equals an accomplished Communist Commonwealth – in which bounty, "to each according to his needs," is poured from a horn of plenty.

Most questionable about myth is the myth that something is true because something is sacred.

Business, too, has its myths. There is the "invisible hand," for example, which Adam Smith said would find the way for rich men to "divide with the poor the product of all their improvements," and would thereby efficiently and beneficially "promote an end which was no part of their intention."[10] And yet, as Adolf Berle and Gardiner Means said in 1993[11] and Alfred Chandler Jr. in 1977,[12] the invisible hand of ownership has become weaker, while the hands of management control are stronger, more intentional, and more visible.

Many business people and economists also believe the myth that business cycles are inevitable. But there is no repetition of the past through predestined cycles. There are economic swings that have nothing to do with cycles. Economies indeed undershoot and overshoot; industries undershoot and overshoot; corporations undershoot and overshoot; waves of optimism and pessimism happen; warns occur; unforeseen political events take place; expectations become too high or too low; there is a lack of new technologies of promise; there is a shortage or a glut of some fuel or commodity; there are false compositions of individual judgements; governments pursue inflationary or disinflationary policies too vigorously or too long; banks and financial institutions lend too exuberantly or too reluctantly; there is no "inducement to invest," or no "propensity to consume."

It is implausible that events which are unique in their time should add up to fate, fixed patterns, loops, regularities and replications. Things rise and things fall. But there is no predetermined pattern which commands that they shall do so recurringly. To blame slumps and recessions on "inevitable" business cycles is often to excuse national or global policy failures.

Progress and Science: Uncertain Certainties

Julian Huxley has listed historical myths as examples of brakes on progress: tribal ritual, recurring preoccupations with sin in Christianity, symbols and analogies in the Middle Ages, the glorification of the state in fascism, the racialism of egregious patriots, the caste system in many nations and tribes, the Divine Right of Kings.[13] In ancient Egypt, for example, in Heian and later feudal Japan, in Europe in the Middle Ages, in Russia until at least the middle of the 19th century, the common people were firmly shackled to unalterable stations. Societies of this kind, frozen in their molds, did not beget the idea of progress. They could dream of heaven but not of heaven on earth. Common to all these arrangements was that none thought itself mistaken.

Two forces exist which, by their nature, break such old molds: business and science. Both gain strength from deepening insights: when science makes new findings, business profits from them.

On a practical level science and business are good allies. But the spirit of science is changing. In prospect, science may be certain of nature's constancy, but no longer seems certain of its own certainties. The march of science is exhilarating, but ultimate horizons are receding. New irregularities are described. Matter and energy transmute one into the other. Particles are waves, waves are particles; they weave and dance together in the transvestite waltz of fundamental physics. The empyrean of stars is more a wary balance between enormous tensions than a celestial carpet of tranquillity. One immutability of nature mutates into the next. Are things behind a veil, a curtain, or a wall?

Scientists are honest about it; all physical theories, they admit, are approximations of reality which can fail if pushed too far. The eminent physicist Stephen Hawking even goes so far as not to demand that theory correspond to reality because "I don't know what [reality] is." He is humbly content that theory correctly predicts the results of measurements.

Shortly before J.B. Bury wrote his *Idea of Progress*[1] in 1932, a major change had occurred in our view of scientific certainty and the fixity of nature. Bury could then still say that science, more than anything else, had helped us to transcend the illusion of the finality of progress. He could not say that now without qualification.

Science has been man's most successful endeavor. The application of science and technology to everyday life has brought immense material progress. But science is no longer, as Bury was then still able to suppose, one of the undoubted carriers of the *idea* of progress.

In 1927, Heisenberg proclaimed the "uncertainty principle." So far as its observers are concerned, some natural phenomena can seem to act indeterminately; science can no longer, except with varying degrees of statistical accuracy, make definite predictions on how subatomic particles will behave in certain circumstances. The principle of complementarity ordains that it is impossible to measure both the position *and* the velocity (or momentum) of a particle simultaneously. If one is determined the other remains vague. In the seventy years since Heisenberg (and Schrödinger, who in 1924 said that fundamental particles may also be wave-like), no experiment has disproved indeterminacy. Fuzz, it seems, is part of nature.

Uncertainty and unpredictability are only manifest at the atomic level or below. But this is the level which computers are fast approaching. And if computers are fast approaching this limit, could the human brain perhaps have reached it long ago? If so, we may perhaps ourselves be indeterminate or statistical reasoners.[14] Why do we approximate well, yet are mediocre at exactness?

And though indeterminacy manifests itself in the very small, it calls into question the measure of smallness. How small is small? Is smallness bounded? How big is big? How long is a (cosmic) string? Is infinity bounded, too? Can we be sure that indeterminacy does not exist on some vast scale elsewhere – at a level of vastness, perhaps, which is in turn very small compared with even greater vastnesses beyond?

Even mathematics, that most consistent and certain of sciences, is no longer proof against uncertainty. In 1931, Kurt Gödel said that in any logical mathematical system there are questions which cannot be proved or disproved within the axioms and assumptions of that system. To the distress of Bertrand Russell, who, together with Alfred North Whitehead, had written that monument to human intelligence called the *Principia Mathematica* some two decades earlier, Gödel showed that a logico-mathematical system can be complete, or can be consistent; but not both complete *and* consistent. It cannot be certain, Gödel claimed, that the basic axioms of arithmetic will not give rise to contradictions. The pure, Platonic nature of mathematics endured for less than one generation.

Here is a sentence from Stephen Hawking's *A Brief History of Time*: "There is no ultimate theory of the universe, just an infinite sequence of theories that describe the universe more and more accurately." He adds, a little less than forcefully, that science might conceivably find a complete description of the universe. But that, too, he says, would be a theory, and while theories can be falsified, "theories can't be proved."[15]

Progress believes, as it must, that things will improve. Of this, science is skeptical: it does not follow that because things become known – given that enough information inheres in them to make them knowable – they become better. Science does not rectify the world; it only rectifies itself.

In the epilogue to *The First Three Minutes*,[16] in one of the most poignant passages ever written on the fate of man, the physicist Stephen Weinberg concludes that the present universe faces ineluctable extinction in endless cold or intolerable heat. The more comprehensible the universe becomes, the more pointless it seems. "[T]he effort to understand the universe is one of the very few things that lifts life a little above the level of farce, and gives it some of the grace of tragedy."

Is reassurance to be found amid the apparent wobbliness of nature? The history of science tells of an ever greater universe far beyond earth as pivot of the universe; of a creation so vast that man is dwarfed and diminished; but so great a work, also, that its creator is enhanced to majesty and mystery beyond imagination. But this creation seems far removed from cosmic kindliness: it is a universe of endless cold, insufferable heat, empty, its silences punctuated by disasters. A universe so impersonal that we are thrown back to the only harbour we know: the knowledge of ourselves. "Men, almost certainly, are capable of more than they have so far achieved. But what they achieve ... will be a consequence of their remaining anxious, passionate, discontented beings. To attempt, in the quest for perfection, to raise men above that level is to court disaster: there is no level above it, there is only a level below it."[17]

And even if science were to find a unifying theory to explain the rules of the celestial game, it will only have answered *how*. It will not have answered Leibniz's Why – why is there something rather than nothing; what is the purpose of creation? "If we find the answer to that," says Stephen Hawking, "it would be the ultimate triumph of human reason – for we would then know the mind of God."

No, we wouldn't, even then. We would only know the one magnificent manifestation He gave us as our enormous neighborhood. And even when, and even if, we shall have uncovered the deepest design of the universe, and even when, and even if, we shall have an ultimate theory of matter, space, time, energy, life, intelligence and consciousness, we shall not be any nearer to man's tranquillity or the love of his neighbor.

Business has lived with this confusion of meaning and of purpose and yet has remained hopeful. It made progress where there seemed to be no progress. By turns generous and greedy, adaptable and stiff, radical and reactionary, open-minded and self-seeking, it has, by fate and by its nature, been an agent of improvement in spite of the rooted institutions of society. It gave meaning where there seemed to be no meaning. Enterprise always found it more satisfactory, and in the end more fruitful, to create new meanings than to receive uncritically, and obey unquestioningly, old meanings imposed by establishments of power. Without science, what would we have of industry? And without industry, what would we have of science? Business found it more satisfactory and fruitful to give the world the serviceability of printed books, telephones, drains and sanitation, piped gas and water, television, warm clothes and comfortable bedding. To give the world these, and through them more dignity, has been the implicit purpose of business enterprise. No need to argue, then, whether business is the main carrier of the idea of progress. Business makes it happen.

Business invented the new space in which it works: economic space, which puts few demands on physical dimensions. It also compressed time: the distance of a telephone agreement between New York and London is the cost of the call and fractions of a minute.

Summary

About half a century ago belief in the boundlessness of the world and its resources began to be abandoned – and with it hopes of the automatic certainty of progress.

Progress is a duty. Little is gained by analogies from nature and from Darwinian parallels, because civilization is a "checking of the cosmic process at every step." But social myths – such as established and "divine" rights, hierarchies of class, sainted prejudices and "invisible hands" – have ruled the world for far too long. None thought itself mistaken, yet each one was.

At the fringes of science now are curious uncertainties; but at its middle is enormous fruitfulness which business knows and uses. Corporations, like individuals, "are capable of more than they have so far achieved. But what they achieve ... will be a consequence of their remaining anxious, passionate, discontented beings." It's up to us.

Capitalism has been defined as an economic-cultural system, organized economically around the institution of property. The next chapter turns to that institution.

3

Capitalism and the Idea of Fair Property

> **"**The rationale of human society is based upon this general and simple principle: I want to be happy; but I live with men who, like myself, want to be happy as well, each according to his own light: let us then search for the means of procuring our happiness by procuring theirs or at least without ever harming it. **"**
>
> Article on "Man" (*Homme*) in Diderot's *Encyclopédie* (1751–1780)

Why a chapter about property in a book on corporations, conviction and the real business of capitalism? Because the modern concept of property is grounded in a concept of justice. Capitalism, in turn, is based on property and property exchanges. Therefore capitalism is based on an accommodation with social justice.

Property is only remotely a "natural" concept. If, on the one hand, all property were "naturally" state property, then private justice would be silenced; if, on the other, private property were "naturally" an absolute dominion, then the sole owner of a source of water would be free to leave all others thirsty, and keeping slaves would be a right of property. Because of justice, neither is the case.

Two levels of justice are involved. The first is simple: I pay you, and you give me an equivalent in goods or services. No other justice is obviously involved. The other is less simple and less amenable to logic or reason. It is the effect of the capitalist process on society. Therefore capitalism ultimately depends on acceptably just and generous results.

Business is primarily a practical application of property relationships, of what is mine and what is yours, of what it owes and what is owed to it, of what it offers and in return expects. In these relationships business is circumscribed by rules and laws. Everything else it does is art, creation, choice and reasonable freedom.

The idea of property as now established is still a contentious work in progress and is still deeply rooted in its history. And yet, mine and yours remain closer to right and wrong than to any axioms of accountancy. Which is why mine and yours are examined in the context of civilized markets.

Capitalism and the Idea
of Fair Property

The Maze of "Property"

Beware of "simple" principles. Simple principles are rarely simple. They wriggle. They have complex applications, and their simplicity fans out into a multiplicity of slippery meanings.

Property and its "irritating pedigree of ideas" is one such "simple" principle. A prime assertion that "private property is right" soon leads to infinite, passionate and long debate on "what is property?" and "what is private?" and "what is right?" and why.

Like particles in physics, property initially appears to concern material objects. It then reappears as waves of energy in which the push-me-pull-you of my claims on you, your claims on me, our claims on several of you, and your claims on us, begin to behave like the strong, weak, electromagnetic and gravitational forces of nature; to which must be added (quantum) indeterminacy when the principles are so caught in webs of ambiguity that rights of property, liberty, ownership, possession and control become indefinite and blurred. Or they become so entangled in a confliction of laws that, like the collision of matter with anti-matter, they destroy each other and leave only a sucking vacuum behind.

In *Ancient Law* (1861), Sir Henry Sumner Maine, a great

jurist of the 19th century, tried to explain the origins of property by supposing that the first proprietor was probably a "strong man armed who kept his goods in peace." But why was it, he asked, that the long continuance of the institution of property created a sentiment of respect for possessions? Somehow, he answers, "its true basis seems to be, not an instinctive bias towards the institution of Property, but a presumption ... that *everything ought to have an owner.*" But this sort of argument is unfortunately circular.

Other than the argument that things have owners because they ought to have them, what justification does anyone have for saying that something is his (or hers, or a corporation's)?

How can one tell whether he (she, or it) owns something justly? Does someone who "deserves" to own his property have a better claim to ownership than someone else who does not "deserve" to own it? Is there a difference between "active" property (that, say, of a working corporation) and "passive" property (that, say, of a landlord who inherited his property from several earlier generations)?

What kind of distribution of wealth is either fair or efficient or desirable, and why? Is human inequality in any sense a justification for an inequality of riches?

Is there only one satisfactory justification for property, or are there several justifications? If there are several justifications, are they compatible with each other?

Is it right for property to be disposable by holders of trust and power (like corporation managers) or only by beneficial holders of equity (like shareholders)?

Is there a sense in which the idea of property is "natural," or are the laws of property only a set of conventions to govern "bundles of [economic] power?" Or put it this way: Is the institution of property founded on "natural" law, or on positive, man-made law? Or on a mix of these? If a small conifer is hung with baubles, tinsel, angels, candles and colored paper stars, is it still a natural object or is it a Christmas tree?

What answers have been given to these questions in the past, and what answers may be given to them in the future?

The meanings of "have" cover more than five pages in the Oxford English Dictionary. In the 4,000 years from the ancient Babylonian codes of law (1792–1750 BC) until today, life, lawyers and legislators have split, refined, subdivided and multiplied the meaning of possession.

"Possessions" suggests solid objects – land, houses, cattle, wells, trees, gold, coins. But even in ancient and early law "things" were not what they seemed to be. One authority, the 20th-century jurist Frederick Pollock, elegantly calls a thing "some possible matter of rights and duties, conceived as a whole and apart from all others." Another says simply that "property rights always define relations between men, not between men and material objects."[1]

"Sovereign" institutions – congresses and parliaments, sometimes dictators and kings – have the *imperium*, or rights of regulation for the uses of things; and having made the rules, pass on the rights of "dominion" or ownership to the members of the public. These rights may be for absolute *dominium*, as in the days of the Roman Republic in which it was said that Brutus could condemn his own son to death and receive the plaudits of his peers.

Or the dominion may be highly qualified; it may be for tangible and corporeal or intangible and incorporeal things, wholly "owned" things or things shared in common, fungible (replaceable in kind) things or non-fungible (unique) things, private or corporate things, real property or personal property, *immobilia* or *mobilia*, real property or goods and chattels, formal property or informal property, freely held *alod* or conditionally held *feud*. "Good will" becomes a property, being the present value put upon the expected beneficial actions of other people. And as to taxes, accumulated losses can also be a valuable property.

The apportionment of property has not historically been fair. In his enquiry into the causes of the wealth of nations, Adam Smith had good reason to remark that it has generally been the policy of rulers to make wealth secure and "to defend the rich from the poor." Such was the case – and it was only one of many – when the feudal lords of the Middle Ages held their own courts, were judges in their own cause, and pumped up their own powers while hearing their tenants' complaints.

It has even been said that judiciaries do not protect property; but rather that "they called that property to which they accorded protection."[2]

"Neither Steal Nor Covet"

Only negative definitions of the idea of private property are to be found in ancient texts. Exodus in the Old Testament commands "Thou shall *not* steal" and "Thou shall *not* covet . . . anything that is thy neighbour's." Now, to say that it is wrong to deprive a neighbor of his things presupposes that some prior and unquestioned rights to property prevailed in biblical times.

Thus, if the institution of private property existed, as it would appear to have done for as long as men have lived in community, then at least six things seem to me to follow:

First, *exclusiveness*: If ownership is right, it must also be right for the owner to be immune from any deprivation of what is his. Therefore ownership, as well as being an *in*clusion, is also an *ex*clusion. "In short, the change in the concept of property from physical things to the exchange-value of things is a change from a concept of holding things for one's own use to withholding things from others' use."[3]

Second, *separation in time*: Exclusion through ownership is a way of preventing inconvenient concurrence. No two or more persons or entities may independently and simultaneously hold the same land, plough with the same ox, hold the reins of the same horse, sit on the same chair, eat the same slice of bread, have the same wife, be the same child's father, be author of the same book, and so on. Patents and copyrights, for example, are more an allotment of property rights in time than in space.

Third, *social acceptance*: For rights of ownership to exist, they must be admitted not only by those who own, but also by those who do *not* own. In a free society, either a social consensus must exist about the acceptability of property rights; or people must be unquestioning about the *status quo*; or there must be enough popular ignorance for people to tolerate inequities of ownership and possession as a "natural" order of things; or else there must be, as under despots, no possibility of debate at all.

Fourth, *social definition*: By categories, the Romans defined most things as being outside commerce and only one thing as being within the private domain. In the Roman digests of law, these were the categories and sub-categories: common things like air (*res communes*); divine things like nature, which belong to nobody (*res nullius*). Then there were sacred things like temples (*res sacrae*); religious things like burial grounds (*res religiosae*); sanctified things like city walls (*res sanctae*); public things like ports, streets and public monuments (*res publicae*); then came things like theatres, racecourses, and slaves in public service (*res universitatis*); and, lastly, came the category of things in the domain of private property (*res singulae*).

Had a classification of property been made only three or four centuries ago, these Roman categories might still have been appropriate to the structures of the Western world. Things "sacred or religious" would still have been deemed holy. In some countries it would have caused no surprise had slaves in public service been accounted for as public assets. Air and water were still free and mostly pure except in cities; and while there were few lands in Europe that were not in someone's possession, there were more than enough of the *res nullius* of nature and its bounty in the remaining world available for capture from its native peoples. An entire continent, now Australia, was declared a *res nullius* by Britain on the grounds than its aboriginal peoples were savage and legally incompetent.

Now, however, things which "belong" to nobody have come under someone's guardianship. From the 19th century onward it became current dogma that nothing can be without possessor, or, if in the charge of governments, without protector. Things that have been put beyond commerce by the law have been slotted into some government domain or other. The reality that modern commerce has greatly broadened obscures the fact that the state's policing has greatly widened.

To the classical categories of property – ownership and possession – a third, never new except in the fancy of "free" market theorists, has again gained force: *de facto* control divorced from rights of property. Control of property rights has again become a third form of property. Courts of law have long been more concerned with who has the better title to the control of a thing than who is the owner of it. Managers have for a long time governed corporations without being particularly concerned about non-controlling equity-holders.

National ownership of the "commanding heights of the economy," too, is ceasing. It not only proved unnecessary for control, but in fact hindered it. Governments were blamed for the cost and frequent lack of performance of nationalized industries or entities. They could not easily increase capitalization, because capital came from involuntary taxpayers, not voluntary lenders, investors and share buyers. Governments rediscovered that they did not have to own industries to be able to make them obey financial disclosure, reporting, ecological, physical, ethical or safety standards, and standards of responsibility for product fitness and endurance. States as sovereigns

discovered that control by command was enough. So was "managed," "directed," "regulated" or "structured competition," *Sozialmarktwirtschaft* or "a social market economy."

Overarching legal control by regulation is gaining. In August 1994, an English High Court judge made a ruling in the case of water utilities which had once been publicly owned but had since been privatized. Their legal form, he said, was irrelevant; it was also irrelevant that they were commercial concerns and not agents of the state. It was however relevant that they were, in a social sense, "emanations of the state." The real question was not whether the state had managerial control, but whether the *public service in question* was within the control of the state.

Fifth, **social inequality**: A system may arise (and did) in which, while there is equality before the law, there is inequality of rewards. The stability of such a society will, likewise, depend on the degree of consent, acceptance, sufferance and acquiescence of the public. "This is not to say that inequality of reward and equality before the law cannot coexist, but it is to say that philosophies of social justice must be taken with a pinch of salt, because, when complete equality becomes an irresistible force, complete justice immediately becomes an immmovable object."[4]

A society based on the "free" acquisition of property is a society in which a compromise between wealth on the one hand and adequate fairness on the other has been struck and accepted – fully by a few, and warily by the many who may feel that property as a principle intrudes on fairness as a principle.

These many might argue that justice should concern itself not only with a person's right to own, but also with *how much* a person may decently own. The Bible forestalls this argument by telling us not to covet anything that is our neighbor's – whether he is rich or poor; and also, the law is primarily concerned with who has the right to possess, not how much is possessed; who has the better title, not how much the title is worth. No court of law, for example, anywhere determines the *scale* of tax that rich and poor must pay to the state; nor does it determine the *scale* of payments they may receive from it when unemployed, or old, or sick. Decisions on these matters are not for courts of law to make, but by the holders of sovereign rights: the state.

Sixth, **derived power**. Much of the power which comes with ownership is *indirect*. The intention of the Coca-Cola and PepsiCo corporations is to sell soft drinks; the intention of the McDonald's and Burger King corporations is to sell burgers. But these corporations have become world "capitalist cultural" phenomena – symbols of something they did not set out to be. They gained these powers more by accretion than by intention.

If such are the derived powers of individual corporations, what is to be made of the derived powers of business in the aggregate? It cannot be said that this immense accretion of power and influence is intended by the world of business. It is not. It arises naturally when a sufficient increase in quantity brings with it a change in quality. Business now shapes the ways of the world and many of the conditions, public and even intimate, in which we live our lives. Shall derived powers be seen as implicit in the concept of property, or are they just fortuitous? Do the derived powers of business require separate consideration, separate curbs and separate licenses?

Society's answer is plain. Legal rights of property may be fully exercised – up to a point. That point is reached when the intrusion bites. It then begins to matter whether the powers of property are fair.

The rest of the chapter considers this in the light of the question whether past debate was simply about the ownership of property, or whether it was mainly about power, including the social control of power.

The Arguments for Equality

Is there a sense in which the idea of property is *natural*? Equality is, of course, a much simpler, more specific and more coherent idea than liberty: it simply means the same for each. The Romans, leaning on the opinions of ancient Greeks, said that "that which is equal and good is the law of laws." (The sentiment, though proclaimed, went unpracticed by them.)

Liberties, however, are not coherent. Each liberty is separate from every other liberty; one liberty may clash with another liberty. Equality leads in one direction – equality; whereas liberty and "free enterprise" can lead in any and in many directions. What guides liberties (including the freedom to own and manage property) to good destinations?

It is not from convention that dogs will naturally fight over a bone, or that babies will naturally grasp for toys, or that men will quickly dip their snouts into unguarded troughs full of the "stinkings of waters of self-interest." Man is inclined to take, take without requitement, and reap where he did not sow.

Yet we know the difference between dogs and sensible people. Sensible people "naturally" expect requitement from others, and these others, equally naturally, expect requitement from sensible people. If there is one concept which is "naturally" understood by man it is the idea of reciprocity – the idea, namely, that if I have the right to want, another also has it. St Thomas Aquinas, in the 13th century, thought this perception innate, and named it fellow-feeling, synderesis. Adam Smith, in the 18th century, spoke of the "impartial spectator" within us, akin to a dispassionate conscience. Sigmund Freud, in the 20th century, may have had this in mind when he called it the super-ego. The high apotheosis of this human recognition is the command to love your neighbor as yourself – to treat him not as nature treats him, but *as you should if you were nature.*

Somehow, as between the one and the other, the grab and the let, the give and the take, the rights of property settled. Property has at heart little to do with "natural" rights. It has much to do with self-regard tempered by an understanding of reciprocity admitted by the law. For instance, though the prevailing theory of his day based property on "natural" rights,

Thomas Jefferson, in 1816, wrote a letter to Du Pont de Nemours in which he said that the "right to property is founded in our natural wants ... without violating the similar rights of other sensible beings." There was no mention of "natural" rights.

At any rate, as now established, the principles of justice are not so much concerned with the right to own, but with the proper and sufficiently sociable uses of that which is owned or managed.

The Arguments for Inequality

Now the difficulty with the argument that property rights are "natural" is that, to be doubly natural, they must also be equal. Property may be all right, but it is not evident by what natural right some may have more than others. Put another way, what kind of "right" can it be that entitles some to *less* wealth than others? Rights to property cannot justify full bowls of soup for some and blank spoons for others. They cannot even justify great libraries and museums.

And so, to justify an unequal distribution of the world's goods, other arguments become necessary – and there are many of them, starting of course with the unsociable fact that there is more excitement in becoming unequally richer than in being equally rich. Few business people are unaware of this exuberant sentiment.

As the fate of the Soviet system has shown, the strongest arguments from experience are, one, that keeping citizens equal is too complicated, even in theory; and, two, that paradoxically, strong efforts to enforce equality tend to favour inequality. If talent, including entrepreneurial talent, is not allowed to rise to the top, there must be someone to stop it from ascending. Titled and untitled comissars are found to push rising heads under water, and hammer down protruding nails.

Education is an example of the incongruity of equality with inequality. Nearly everyone agrees that education is a universal good and that all children have an equal right to schooling. Yet, since natural promise is unequal, nearly everyone also agrees that talented children will learn more, and will have a better chance to gain many of life's preferments – including greater wealth and ampler property. An *initial equal right* to education *is not the path to subsequent equality*. The argument must therefore be shifted to quite another plane: though education increases inequality, it does lend some dignity to all. The dignity which comes with the ability to read, write and count is still a universal good apart from, and beyond, equality or inequality.

Where a society inclines more to *individual* liberty, an inequality of property tends to follow, because, if any man has a right to his property, a rich man also has it. Whereas when *equality* of property is put above civil liberty, actual equality may follow, or it may not. On the whole, it does not follow, and, on the whole, equality only works between monastic friars.

The impracticability of equality was one argument. There was another. Since it was not possible to justify unequal rights to property by reason alone, mankind employed a device often used to make inconclusive arguments conclusive: it provided them with haloes and endowed them with sanctity. Kings and their vassals were granted a holy glow by the "natural" right of conquest or the "Divine Right of Kings."

The argument for sacred privilege was withdrawn by the Enlightenment. With greater humanity but nearly the same degree of beatitude, it was instead argued that "all men ... have certain natural, essential and inalienable rights; among which may be reckoned the right of ... acquiring, possessing, and protecting property ..."[5] This argument assumed that "natural" law and natural justice somehow existed as a "brooding omnipresence in the sky"(Justice Oliver Wendell Holmes's phrase) and were sacred without the need for further proof.

The Arguments for Natural Rights

The problem with "natural" laws and "natural" rights is that they seem natural some of the time and far-fetched at others. One cannot, for example, derive principles for the operation of a stock exchange from the simple dictum "follow nature," or even "follow ideal nature." Unlike of persons, it cannot be said of corporations that they have a "natural" right to exist. It would indeed be laughable to claim that founding a corporation is based on its natural right to be founded. Yet once it has been founded, Maitland says, "it often struck me that morally there is most personality where legally there is none."

Modern jurists of the very highest eminence, such as America's Chief Justice Cardozo and Oliver Wendell Holmes before him, were not advocates of the Law of Nature. Yet, Cardozo said, "it is the stuff out of which human or positive law is to be woven, when other sources fail." Judges, he said, seek from within the positive law "its ideal, and its enduring idea." He cites the French Civil Code which indirectly commends recourse to natural law when all else fails. Its 4th article states that a judge who refuses to judge on the pretext that the law is silent, obscure or inadequate, may himself be culpable of a denial of justice. Also culpable under the Code are inert bystanders who make no effort to save a drowning person.

But even the Middle Ages had a practical problem with "natural" law: while it was divine law, and as such infallible, there was no infallible way of knowing what it was. And so one must conclude that the conflicts between a "natural" sense of fairness and the practical need for "law and order" will never disappear in human society.

What Makes Property "Fair Property?"

The history of "natural" law is long. Although it has been called an "empty bottle decorated with a nice label," it has also been called an "innate property of all men," a "criterion of absolute justice," a "means of distinguishing just from unjust laws," and, in the perennial view of the Roman Church, reaffirmed in 1891, "the same thing as eternal law, implanted in rational creatures, and inclining them to their right action and end; and can be nothing else but the eternal reason of God."[6]

One century later the Pope reasserted[7] that man, *through the labor by which he has gained it*, has a natural right to property. But it is a qualified right concerning which "a most strict account must be given [by men] to the Supreme Judge for the use of all they possess." The dictate of natural law commands, so says his Church, that business owes man something beyond mere business, by "reason of his lofty dignity." Among Protestants too, from Luther's friend Philip Melanchthon in the 16th century to Jacques Ellul in the middle of the 20th, the debate persists that the right to (and of) property is founded on, and bounded by, divine or natural law.[8]

The view that man has a natural right to property through the labor by which he has gained it brings the opinion of the Christian Church into ironic similarity with John Locke (1632–1704), with Adam Smith (1723–1790) and, absurdly, with Karl Marx (1818–1883).

The heart of Locke's argument was that man had a property in his own person and labor; and that this labor, when applied and mingled with a bit of nature, made that bit of nature his own. The Romans called this the mode of "natural acquisition." Similarly, Adam Smith held that the property which every man has in his own labor was the original foundation of all other property, and was thus sacred and inviolable.

This eventually led to the Labor Theory of Value of which Marx and his heirs made excellent use for more than a century. Capitalists, they said, for their own enrichment and convenience, unfairly withhold some of the "surplus value" created by workers, and must not.

This irony was added to others. In the first place Locke's view came at a time when the factory system began to grow, and when parcelling land in proportion to the labors of its tiller became a piece of rural romance.

In truth, the idea that value is equal to the amount of labor stored in a "thing" does not work. Ditch-digging may be measurable; but what is the labor-value that went into $E = mc^2$?

It was once thought – by William Blackstone in his 18th century *Commentaries on the Laws of England,* for example – that laws and rules "naturally" pre-exist. The task of judges is to find them. It is now more common to accept that life audits law, and not that law audits life. "Law," so to speak, "never *is,* but is always about to be."

Money having become the common medium, the minglings of the marketplace made the fruits of labor anonymous. They would no longer be seen as the fruits of this one sturdy laborer's tree. Locke, to be sure, was aware of the alteration which the reality of money made to his views. He modified the "natural rights" argument for property and allowed that man-made, conventional law ruled the ordering of affairs "by compact and agreement."

But what does *equal* labor mean? Equal amounts of labor may have been expended in writing a Shakespeare sonnet or a lewd limerick; in assembling a piece of expensive software or writing a boring sermon; in managing a giant corporation or being its mailman; in patenting a profitable left-hand widget or in devising the theory of relativity. The determination of value through its content of work or effort is a good measure for oxen, slaves and machines; but it is a rubber band when used to measure human achievement.

Property Justified by Its Social Utility

Any social arrangement must have two qualities: it must be effective and must be acceptable. Property is not one of the ends of civilization; it is one of the means to it. If it is not that, or cannot be made that, there is no point in it. Arguments about property rights must in the end rest not on sanctifiability but on justifiability.

But even if we take justifiability to be the criterion, should it be moral justifiability alone, or justifiability on the grounds of usefulness? And if on grounds of usefulness, do we choose to prefer the advancement of utility to the community, or do we choose to prefer the advancement of individual liberties regardless of community? Or perhaps a salad made of both? (I did warn against the deceptive simplicity of "simple" ideas. The salad becomes very mixed indeed in times of war, when "community" overrides "individual," even in democratic countries.)

"Utility," more than "use," suggests a public purpose. One of the earliest arguments for a utilitarian view of property was St Augustine's (354–430 AD) when he write in one of his letters that that was possessed rightly which was possessed justly, and that that was possessed justly which was possessed well; but that which was badly used was badly possessed (since it had no utility for others).

In the early 18th century, property was justified by a doctrine of "natural" rights. The late 18th and 19th century instead developed utilitarianism as a doctrine which would "procure the greatest happiness for the greatest number."

Enter a progression towards the state and towards socialism. David Hume, who died in 1776, held that "all questions of property are subordinate to [the] authority of civil laws." Which also meant, so one of Hume's contemporaries, Joseph Priestley, thought, that *the state might revoke* rights to property if these rights were contrary to the public interest. Here, then, enters the first progression: towards the state.

Then came the mature factory system, early mass-production, and John Stuart Mill. Mill, who died in 1873, nearly a century after Hume, still battled with natural rights *versus* utility.

But whereas for Hume "property procures the greatest *happiness* for the greatest number," for Mill property procures the greatest *horn-of-plenty* productivity for the greatest number (see Chapter 1). Utilitarianism was also compatible with democracy: if a proposed action scores more useful and commendable points than another, then, as in counting votes at an election, let the majority prevail. This attitude entrenched itself in the English-speaking world; it brought mild socialism, American pragmatism, and the political humanitarianism of the welfare state.

Progression to New Emperors: the State, and Socialism

The Continental progression was more turbulent.

Hegel died in 1831. *Volksgeist*, the spirit of peoplehood, suffused German thinking after Germany's liberation from Napoleon. At that time, the historical study of "real law as the proper will of the people" had been proclaimed by F.K. von Savigny, a learned German scholar of Roman and medieval law. Note the word "will."

Following Kant who had died in 1804, property, Hegel said, arises when a person's *will* (rather than his labor) is directed to the domination of an inanimate object with no will of its own. Such an exercise of the individual will is an expression of human freedom. If the ownership of things were shared, or if property were held in common, this freedom would be limited, confused, or frustrated. Therefore private, individual property is justified. The Labor Theory of Value was wrong since it could not justify the ownership of land – land being not a product of labor but *sui generis*, a thing apart, not created by man. So it could not be labor, but only the direction of the freedom of the will upon it which could justify the appropriation and ownership of land.

Now came a Hegelian twist in the logic of this first argument. The individual is not alone. Collectives – families, corporations, and above all the state – share a common will and embody a common spirit which is superior to the will of individuals (an idea somewhat like Rousseau's invention of the "general will"). The existence of the state and the protection it offers makes it possible for individuals to live in conditions in which they can exercise their freedom of will. Therefore the state has a superior claim. It proclaims a body of law. "The state," said Hegel, "is the world which mind has made for itself; ... As high as mind stands over nature, so high does the state stand above physical life. Man must therefore venerate the state as a secular deity," as "earthly divine."[9]

But now, having taken with one hand, Hegel gave back with the other: since it is in the interest of the state to allow the exercise of individual wills, it is also in the interest of the state to allow private property by law.

The preeminence of the state had been established. One path, the path to Naziism, was paved by those who ignored Hegel's advocacy of individual rights and who emphasized the primacy of the state. Another path led to Marxian–Engelsian communism.

As to this, in France Pierre-Joseph Proudhon wrote "What is Property?" in 1840, shortly after Hegel's death. His motto was "I Destroy and I Build" – which half fixes the tenor of his thoughts. For Proudhon, the product of labor belongs to the laborer. But the entanglement of industry makes separation of each man's contribution impossible; hence all must share equally, and property must be regarded as a common social good in a communism of equal esteem.

With the typical generosity of the exclusive prophet, Marx first praised Proudhon's "What is Property?" in 1840, only to condemn him a few years later as an idealist.

Marx and Engels argued that societies had originally lived in community and had owned things together. This was nullified or "negated" by the rise of private ownership. What had to be done was to "negate the negations" (Hegel's phrase), nullify the nullification, and put things back into their proper places. Capital must be brought into public ownership under the guardianship of the proletariat.

History was reinterpreted by Marx, usury was declared still wrong, and the Labor Theory of Value was restored. Since it was difficult to establish the value of individual labor accurately, the ultimate solution was creation-in-common but reward in accordance with the *needs* of each individual. But, alas, so impossible is it to separate "I need" from "I want" that it was never seriously tried in the seventy years for which the Soviet system endured.

The Jury Votes by a Majority for Property

It may be true that a society based on the existence of private property is not the best conceivable society, or the most fair, or the most elegant. Some have damned it with faint praise by calling it a society of efficient injustice. But though not a simple society, it is possibly the simplest. First, however tenuously and imperfectly, it takes account of the unequal talents of people and dispenses with preconceived notions about the perfectibility of human nature. Next, the uses of private property make it unnecessary to maintain equality by force. Last though not always, it is vibrant and self-organizing in that there are markets for the creation and free exchange of most forms of property, including ideas.

All this does not imply that the system which grows from private property is conveniently simple. Its legal and social complications are, needless to say, immense. What may be said is that, politically and practically, no other kind of economic fire has yet been lighted which, laid by centuries of history, burns more continuously than the flames of exchange, or more readily changes its heat with newly discovered fuels.

To an extent, it ruthlessly snuffs out its weaker flames and makes ashes of competitors. To an extent, those who most vig-

orously wave the torch of unfettered enterprise often become its
potential subverters and incendiaries. To an extent, also, there is
too great a difference between those who actively tend the fire,
create, and let the world be warmed – which is good; and those
who, having by luck, inheritance or succession become the
keepers of fires lighted by others, warm themselves but shade
their neighbors – which is less good: because it leaves the
question of the feudal privileges of property open to continuing
criticism.

But it is a little more sparing of bureaucracy and offi-
ciousness than any other system. The need to sell to a public, and
not use force to do so, holds corporations tied to the life and
needs of people – however tenuously at times, and however
indirectly. Also, since the innovations of business are incre-
mental rather than revolutionary, they are more easily adapted
and more peaceably absorbed.

Property and the "Pragmatic Sanction" of History

The institution of property and the existence of society are so
interleaved with history and with the daily processes of life that
there is no disentangling the one from the other. We have to
make the best of it; and the task is neither disappointing nor
impossible:

> For we have had no experience of conducting civilized society on
> any other basis, and the waste and friction involved in going to
> any other basis must give us pause. Moreover, whatever we do,
> we must take account of the instinct of acquisitiveness and of
> individual claims grounded thereon. We may believe that the
> law of property is a wise bit of social engineering in the world as
> we know it, and that we satisfy more human wants, secure more
> interests, with a sacrifice of less thereby than by anything we are
> likely to devise – we may believe this without holding that

private property is eternally and absolutely necessary and that human society may not conceivably expect in some civilization, which we cannot forecast, to achieve something different and something better.[10]

Summary and Conclusion

Capitalism depends on the rights of property. Russia, for example, is not now held back by the lack of a bright capitalist dynamic, but mainly by no, or ill-defined, or muddy, rights of property.

Property rights have partly become social rights. Though they have been forged by history, they are not "natural" rights. Nor, except in a formally legal sense, are they the rights of shareholders alone. If these rights are exercised with public approbation, they will endure. If not, they will be changed.

Making profits is one of the rights of property. Profits are applauded when they enhance the wealth of nations and are used for corporate continuance and as offsets to future costs. They are condemned when used intransigently and with disregard for the march of moral history.

Rights of property are the foundation for private gain. They also bring private power with them. Society continues to ask whether private gain confers social gain, and whether private power is harmlessly employed. The question therefore is whether, and how well, the ethos of private success will reconcile with a social ethos of conviction.

4

The Ethos of Success

" The foxes, the little foxes that spoil the vines; for our
vines have tender grapes. **"**

Song of Solomon 2:15

*The Divine Right of Kings and the similar privilege of some nations to
rule over other nations is gone. Few regret its passing. In the course of
the last three centuries faith, too, has turned to puffs of personal
interpretation. What remains?*

*Two value systems arose and persist – the ethos of success and the
ethos of conviction. The aims and objectives of business capitalism – size
power, profit, market share and wealth – are driven by the ethos of
success. All the "virtues" of this world – neighborliness, familiarity,*

faith, hope, justice, charity, fortitude – are vested in the ethos of conviction. Its weakness is that none of these makes money.

The two ethics are often incompatible. The genius of the ethos of conviction rarely inspires the ethos of success. The genius of the ethos of success sometimes impairs the ethos of conviction. There are some exceptions; but these usually cut across each other's grain.

Neither ethos can become the unchallengeable boss: because one makes money, while the other costs money but tells us how to spend it. It is nonsense to think that perfect reconciliations can be found. The ethos of success has an indispensable and exuberant dynamic; and yet we cannot live without a reasonably settled ethos of conviction.

The Ethos of Success

" *Que sais-je?* "
"What do I know?" Michel Montaigne, late 16th century

" *Que suis-je, ou suis-je, ou vais-je, et d'ou suis-je tiré?* "
"What am I, where am I, where go I, whence came I?"
Voltaire, 18th century

" 'How should I live?' 'What should I do?' 'Why should I obey others, and how far?' 'What is freedom, duty, authority?' 'Have I a right to govern myself, or only to be governed well?' 'Is there a purpose which individuals, or societies, or the entire universe, cannot but seek to fulfill? Or are there no such purposes...?' "[1]
Isaiah Berlin, 20th century

The Little Foxes: Ends and Means

Who could possibly have foreseen the shape of the present from the oddnesses of the past, or foresee the shape of the future from the oddnesses of the present? The calculus of future blessings is imprecise. We may guess at the consequences of a plan, but we can hardly guess at the consequences of those consequences.

You can legislate for this and that, regulate here and there, democratize one thing or another, support the helpless and the workless, ameliorate, improve, streamline, make user-friendly, make efficient and cultural and clean, but ideals are not perfectly attainable. Ideals, cloud-like, sometimes carry the thunder of the times; at others, like clouds, they vanish with the age.

In places, pockets of Utopian hopes survive in religious fundamentalism, extreme nationalism, or both. But since an element of viciousness resides in both nationalism and fundamentalism, their Utopias are shot through with contradictions. Whether they themselves understand it or not, their prince, their Machiavelli's "prince" to whom all power, is a mob.

Yet we might agree that a careful choice of reasonable means is more likely to put us on a straight road than awesome ideologies and Utopias. Utopias are suspect. Utopias paint a shining City of God with the pale wash of a single major prejudice. "The Market" is one such present-day Utopian creation – based on a false reading, or non-reading, of Adam Smith. The "market" is neither god nor devil. It is not a devil – which is what Stalin wanted the peoples of the former Soviet Union to believe. It is not a god – which is what many citizens of that lesser Utopia, Orange County, California, believe. But a choice between untempered markets and untempered political power is a bad choice: because the only thing worse than total rule by wavering markets is total rule by willful men.

There are old examples: seeking selective justice, Plato (in the *Laws*) and Aristotle (in the *Republic*) thought well of a kingly class of ruler-guardians, but showed no consideration for slaves, serfs and trade. Marx, too, selectively sought justice, but inverted the order of class preference by approximately 180 degrees.

Over time, unintended consequences usually drown out those that were intended. Ronald Reagan's convictions grew in simple soil. He intended a strong dollar. Within a few years he instead achieved de-industrialization, a weak dollar and a national debt of trillions. With even more passionate conviction, Margaret Thatcher intended a strong economy for Britain. For several years she instead achieved a weakening pound, diminished industry and high unemployment. For many years, Japan intended to go to the limits of mass-production, and did. She has now hit the buffers of invention, and hesitates – it being one thing to pass through the gates of development, improvement and efficiency, but another to make genius hurry. The limits of mass-production as an economy's locomotive may also have now been reached by Germany. But the most egregious example of incompatibility of ends and means was the communist model when in power from Hungary to North Korea. Society is to be more rational, it said; society is to be more simple; society is to be more equal. Instead, what happened to rationality was a false assessment of human longings; what happened to simplicity was tangle; what happened to equality was inequality.

It could hardly have been otherwise. Marxism held that all classes other than the "working" class are parasitical, and that only this class should rule. So, after fulfillment, the situation had to be this: All the members of the *only* class (the surviving proletarian class) are dictators over all the members of the *only* class (the surviving proletarian class). This absurd conflation of ends and means – the "dictatorship of the proletariat" over itself – prevailed for seventy years with the help of policemen.

Acceptable means are more universal, more perennial, less passing, less relative to time and place and circumstance than ends, just as scientific method is more permanent than this or that particular scientific hypothesis. Propriety is an ancient value, and a good king's rule signifies more to his subjects' satisfaction than awesome conquests (but see the "Paradox of the Virtues" below). Some may argue that torture is a means to an end; but only a perverted few would claim that it is an end in itself.

The belief that any means are proper to achieve some supposed and distant good; in short, the belief that ends justify all means, can lead to this: "The whole earth, perpetually steeped in blood, is nothing but a vast altar upon which all that is living must be sacrificed without end, without measure, without pause, until the consummation of things, until evil is extinct, until the death of deaths."[2] There has been enough "ethnic cleansing" to turn this insane early 19th-century opinion into a 20th-century reality. Or it may lead to an absurd reduction in the tyrannical state that George Orwell describes in his novel *1984*: the object of persecution is persecution and the object of torture is torture.

As a businessman I remain persuaded that, with piratical exceptions, profit is the fee received for setting out to do something useful and achieving it. Doubtless love of one's neighbor is a great good in itself. But though less than love, the intention to give trustworthy service is the foundation for life under laws and in commerce. Whatever other good and useful things are done by business, this ranks first and is the source of profit and acceptability.

Now it could be said that the Japanese popular ethos is a collective ethos to which these observations do not apply. On the contrary, the Japanese ethos works in the mass because it starts, not from love, but from individual conduct and a personal sense of obligation (*On*).

It *could* also be said that the Western Christian ethic is older than the Japanese ethos, and that therefore Western foundations have long been laid for high standards of mutual respect and trust. All the foundations indeed exist for high standards of mutual respect and trust. The principles of a moral life are reasonably complete; but their historical practice has been skewed. There were always other ends – conquest, gold, power, empire, property, tribe and nation – which took precedence before Christian, or "christian," norms could be installed.

The Little Foxes: Bad Means for Good Ends

We come to a familiar trap. Is it right to use bad means for good ends or use bad means to avoid worse ends? Is moral choice possible between kind but ineffective means and unkind but effective means? For example, is it right to send people into unemployment and redundancy by installing labor-saving plant and machinery to ensure a competitive future for the corporation? Is there an alternative to this at the level of the firm? Is there an alternative to this at the level of society or nation? Imprisonment of criminals is a costly and unpleasant remedy; but preaching will not always do the job. War was a costly and bloody means to defeat Hitler; but had the Sermon on the Mount been read to him instead, it would scarcely have caused him to sob and abandon his furnaces of hell.

The Paradox of the Virtues is another fox: an excess of any one virtue is itself no virtue. Thrift, if taken to extremes, deprives others of income. The excessive contemplation of beauty leads to the neglect of people. An excess of action destroys caution. Excessive caution leads to inaction. Excessive piety often ends in resignation, which also destroys action. Justice, if taken to extremes, destroys liberty. Liberty, if taken to extremes, destroys justice. "A passion for equality makes vain the hope for freedom."[3] By itself, sincerity is the least of the virtues. Sincerity was not held to be a virtue in ancient times and in the Middle Ages. Truth was the ancient virtue, not sincerity, until late in the 17th century.

In business, too, things are hardly simple. Turning the other cheek is not a business solution, because in business our meekness forwards their attack and their forbearance furthers our encroachment.

There is thus a conflict between an ethos of conviction and an ethos of success. All the virtues – faith, hope, charity, justice, fortitude – are bunched inside the ethos of conviction, but all the great rewards of this world – power and wealth – abide in the ethos of success. Where, in virtue that is its own reward, is profit? Where is the principle that reconciles moral conviction with worldly success? Sadly, no simple reconciling principle is underfoot.

Which is not to say that reconciliation is impossible. No one is ever **in** business in general. He or she is always in **a** business in particular. Every transaction lives in its own new world within the older world. What is right is embedded in what is possible. Principle must be reconciled with the facts of the case for each new situation. Now, this is rarely too difficult since those of us in business already carefully examine means and ends. The history of many long-lived corporations shows that to be shrewd while straight is not only good but useful.

"Let the decision stand" may be a good prejudice in law but it is not a good prejudice in business. There is menace in any one fine old criterion that wraps up all possible decisions in one fine parcel. No single criterion suffices. There are those, for example, who use the corporation's balance sheet as preferred wrapping. Corporations driven by their balance sheets look at the market value of the corporation's assets with unpitying eyes. If realizable assets promise well in the market, the company goes up for sale in parts or in entirety, regardless of achievable future profits, the fate of its employees, or of its incompletely funded pensioners. Other corporations use their profit-and-loss statement for the same purpose. They look at the corporation's current profits and return. They ignore the fact that assets (land, buildings, inventories, but also contingent business opportunities) may be undervalued and stand at outdated acquisition values in the books. Or they may be content to reap high profits for a few years by not replacing, developing or expanding markets, or products, or plant, or machines – or people.

In chess, or in mathematics and science, the ends are given and the means are a matter of aptness. But in human affairs and business *reason and judgement decide the ends* while *reasonableness and conscience must decide the means.*

Until not long ago, the Church prescribed the ends of God as well as God's mystery permitted. People's means towards them lay in virtue and obedience. Since then, many, including David Hume, concluded that reason is the slave of the passions –

their hired gun – whether the passions incline to virtue or to infamy. In either case *it is certain that the "reason" that guides the ethos of success will, at some time, clash with the "reason" that guides the ethos of conviction.* Full justice may be one person's guiding principle; mere effectiveness another's: "Our aims create the light our life is bathed in."[4]

How can we reconcile the two? In simple terms, we must concede that the ethos of success is largely a problem of capitalism and that the ethos of conviction is largely a problem of society. But no solution will be found if the corporation and its managers think that they can adhere to the one without participating in the other.

The Little Foxes: How Much Reason is Reasonable?

Where did Reason lead the modern world?

For the men and women of the 18th century Enlightenment, very broadly, universal "reason" meant that questions of value had objective answers, that these answers were coherent and not in conflict with each other, and that human reason could discover them. The search for them would be long and difficult, but in the end successful. Immanuel Kant proclaimed, in 1785, that one should act only on a maxim that one could *will* to be a universal law *derived from reason*. Such universality would have to exclude incompatible laws – since one could not possibly will a law to become universal which was in contradiction with another universal law. Kant may not have turned to such conclusions had not the Enlightenment kindled the hope that human values could be true, hard, and real.

But under Kant the judge of "universal law" is not dispassion but the human will – a will that is autonomous in judgement, and a will that is a cause-in-itself rather than the servant of nature. Yet "will" as a guide to action is a turn away from classical Enlightenment, which held that universal rules were eternal, not temporal. Still, since Kant said that the will is only free if it conforms to the imperatives of reason-writ-in-heaven, he was, while not a child, at least a brother of the Enlightenment. Nevertheless, as the history of 19th-century Romanticism and 20th-century nationalism has shown, where "will" was king, "reason" became its justifying servant. More on this soon.

The laws of the natural universe connect. There are no parallel but different laws to govern the behavior of nature. There are no two kinds of circle, one more circular than the other. There are no two gravities of which one attracts and the other simultaneously repels. The natural universe is no model for man. There are no moral lessons in the atomic processes of stars. We must maintain the fabric of the world ourselves. We may believe that God, who made all, made the clockwork of the universe; but it is presumptuous to regard Him as a chief mechanic on permanent duty.

People, on the other hand, have painted many portraits of ends and means, pride and humility, good life and better life, beauty, truth, virtue, their alikes or opposites. The tolerant admittance of contending but uncancelled values – pluralism, the open society – is the recognition that in political and economic society even the whitest light is a mix of colors. Acceptable values – in business as in life – are to be found not in a single universal crystal chandelier of reason, but in many. Pluralism, both as a word and as a concept, is a creation of the early 20th century. It is only a little younger than Tolerance which, as is mentioned elsewhere, only found its modern meaning in the early 18th century.

Not only must pluralism tolerate the existence of comprehensive doctrines, it must also tolerate comprehensive and *incompatible* doctrines – religious, moral, and philosophical. That is what the philosopher John Rawls said recently. He asserted that this is only possible in a society which is not only pluralist but also reasonable.[5] Doubtless he is right; but just how far "reasonableness" can stretch remains an unanswered question. Passionate intensity, for one, may overstretch the bow of moderation. And so I suspect that successful pluralism and democracy thrive best in societies of moderate passions and of middling interest in political debate. A little boredom probably helps democracy.

There is also this: business has grown to be a dominant social force in our world – unwittingly and unintentionally. It has also, at least in the West – again unwittingly and unintentionally – made a world which inclines to humanism though it has not yet attained it. If business does not join in this search for humanism wittingly and intentionally it will be out of phase with society; and if it continues to be out of phase, it will continue to come under persistent attack by the rest of society. Now consider a distinction that may not have been made before.

Humanism and Humanitarianism: a Fateful Distinction

The last three centuries have seen humanism (which is about learning and the general dignity of man) and humanitarianism (which is about alleviating the indignity of individual distress) merged and conflated. Humanism is a celebration of man's talents; humanitarianism is a philanthropic love of mankind. The passage from humanism to political humanitarianism was constant, understandable and admirable. But its consequences have been fateful.

Humanitarianism as *public* policy rose in the 19th century. It grew immeasurably in the second half of the 20th century. Bureaucracy and taxes distended with it. The many issues surrounding political humanitarianism are now the most time-consuming and dominant agenda of democratic governments: pensions and retirement benefits, housing, nationally run or financed health services, unemployment compensation, the care of the old, natal and pre-natal care, mental care, safety at work, safe food, safe drugs, safe transportation, foreign aid and much else. With this comes the debate of who shall pay for these, how they shall be paid for and how apportioned.

The proportion of the budget states allot to universities, fundamental research, the arts, sciences and other celebrations of human talents is by comparison slim. Indeed, in the USA and Britain, the parties of the right disdain such purposes for the public domain. Comparatively small sums, no time, nor often inclination, is left for "culture," science and broadmindedness. Welfare issues are constantly on the lips of legislators; but a mention of humanism, rarely made, would have them trot for dictionaries to check on its half-remembered meaning.

In business, the apportioning of "rights" to corporate stakeholders (other than stockholders' legal rights) springs more from a humanist sense of commonwealth than from any general humanitarianism. Corporations are particular institutions and deal with particular groups of people – some small, some, like consumers, large, but still identifiably limited. They are inclined to humanism rather than to political or popular humanitarianism. Its members are interested in humanitarianism as citizens, and that most properly, but as organizations corporations are noticeably uninvolved.

All this is wholly understandable: democracy inclines to populism by its nature; at least let business, the sciences and the arts be humanist. Some managers may say that corporate humanism is not an issue they have ever heard of, and that it's news to them. But it is hardly news to the chairmen and CEOs of large modern corporations in Europe and the United States.

At its simplest, the Renaissance humanism of the 14th and 15th centuries was the transformation of man-as-creation into man-the-creator – rational and autonomous. An idealized ancient

Greece was used for inspiration. Learning became highly valued. Rhetoric, poetry, ethics, history and governance were its curriculum. Ignorance and superstition had no place in this ideal. But no place was found in it for the untutored masses. It was an ideal for the "best" of men and the best in man. It was humanism, but not humanitarianism. Humanism was not opposed to the prevailing order of the world or to its rulers, provided they were guardians of man's talents.

Humanism's continuation was the Enlightenment of the 18th century. It shone with an effulgence of talent brighter than that of almost any other age. On its roll call, whose full recital would overspill a page, were Locke, Hume, Adam Smith, Diderot, Voltaire, Goethe, Kant and Jefferson. But while Diderot's *Encyclopédie* was celebrated in the salons of France, it was still no Sermon-on-the-Mount for multitudes. The "enlightened" despots of Prussia and Russia were not only accepted but applauded. The Enlightenment ideal was still for the "best" of men and the best in man.

And yet humanism inevitably entailed humanitarian expansion. Adam Smith spoke for the miserable poor; Rousseau would cast off the chains that bound all men; Francis Hutcheson recommended compassion and the "love of humanity."

The great conflators of humanism and humanitarianism were the socialists, the social democrats and Christian socialists of the 19th century. At their revolutionary extreme were the French syndicalist-anarchist-libertarian Proudhon and his Russian anarchist friends, the squire Bakunin and the prince Kropotkin; and the unforgiving German communists Marx and Engels. Communists believed in a nationalized economy *and* in a nationalized humanitarianism. The first was to be the economic order; the second was to be the moral order. They were ill-matched.

Now, at the end of the 20th century, business is the great economic orderer. Of the rest, governments, using part of the income of their citizens, are the institutional humanitarians. Churches and governments prescribe or police the moral order with varying degrees of feebleness. Some small but rising funds come from charities and corporate and private bequests, for both humanitarian and humanist purposes. A few universities carry the humanist tradition by ancient inertia. But most of it comes disjointedly from private citizens as a remembered legacy. In the West, political humanitarianism has become conventional and universal. Humanism has become conventional but not universal. Both should be universal in a balanced society.

What is needed is the civilized intent of business and business people to act as practical St Christophers of humanism. Power may then be seen to radiate conscience.

The Unarrested Eye

This is not preaching to the unconverted. The scanning, unarrested eye of the best of major business leaders – the searching eye that makes them leaders – also makes them, in the main, open-minded, humane, skeptical of political dogma, willing to look at reformation, willing to judge by a calculus of social justice as much as of success, hopeful of fair policies by government but often disappointed. Above all, it makes them aware that as it molds itself, business molds the world.

Yet too many lesser leaders of business take a mannered stand and pretend to social toughness. Their calculus is immediate success. They see the market as a playground for profitable forays, and mistakenly equate this with liberty. They do not see profit as reward for service rendered. But they cannot have their cake and eat it. If they believe that they deserve all that they gain, they must also accept that they will deserve all that they may lose.

The traditions of business – discontinuous, to be sure – include an undercurrent of good faith, good works, and tolerance – from industrial Quaker family traditions in England; from Robert Owen's in the textile industry of Britain's North; from Andrew Carnegie's condemnation, in Pennsylvania, of the idolatry of money; from *Walden*, Thoreau's critique of 19th-century greed; to such modern business statesmen as I.S. Shapiro, lately chairman of DuPont, who, in 1984, in *America's Third Revolution*, argued that in addition to freedom and wealth the United States needed better justice and fairer distribution; to Peter Drucker's many writings spread over half a century, and his demonstration that public service, non-profit enterprise, and the time and labor expended in unpaid works and charities by millions of managers and citizens are now a massive segment of the American economy.

Conclusion and Summary

I have argued that business and humanism are not far apart. I have argued that industry and business are by definition in the business of service. I have argued that it is a short step from seeing producer/consumers as sources of wealth to seeing them as resources of commonwealth.

Business people are in a position to decide whether they are privately a party to reasonable universality or only a party to local particularism. In either case, Commodore Vanderbilt's "the public be damned" is out.

5

The Ethos of Conviction

" Man is born a predestined idealist, for he is born to act.
To act is to affirm the worth of an end, and to persist in
affirming the worth of an end is to make an ideal. "
>Justice Oliver Wendell Holmes,
>*Holmes-Pollock Letters*, pp. 181ff

" ... thy sons proclaim thy glorious name by gorry by
jingo by gee by gosh by gum ... "
>ee cummings, *Complete Poems 1904 to 1962*

" Patriotism lies in the nature of man and is something so
self-evident that any exaggeration or emphasis is only
painful or ridiculous, and smothers it instead of
sustaining it. "
>Theodor Haecker, *Journal*, 1939–1944, trans. 1949

" It is the duty of a patriot to prefer ... the interest and
glory of his native country; but a philosopher may be
permitted ... to consider Europe as one great republic,
whose various inhabitants have attained almost the same
level of politeness and cultivation. "
Edward Gibbon, *The Decline and Fall of the Roman Empire*,
1764–1788

*Kant's most famous injunction is essentially this: Act only on the
principle that you would want to become a Universal Moral Law. If a
businessman tried to do so, his conscience would be tattered and torn.*

*Assume that this businessman is a good patriot who loves his
country. Assume also that he is his corporation's chief executive.
Assume further that, having sought and obtained the best advice, he
clearly sees that many of his corporation's assets should be lodged
abroad – in Hong Kong or Timbuctoo – for sound, conservative and
legal business reasons.*

*Regretfully he moves them there, his patriotic feelings notwith-
standing, because it is his duty to his shareholders to do the best he can
for them. If he neglects this obligation the laws of the very country that
he loves may punish him for his omission.*

*Which "universal" moral law is he obliged to heed? A "Universal
Moral Law" for patriot-citizens, or a "Universal Moral Law" for
shareholders' fiduciaries? All of which shows that narrow nationalism is
incompatible with the supranationalism of business in a peaceable
modern world.*

The Ethos of Conviction

> " The foxes, the little foxes that spoil the vines; for our vines have tender grapes. "
> Song of Solomon 2:15

Little Foxes: First Came Reason...

What follows is a sketch of the passage from the Age of Reason to political romanticism and nationalism. It must omit many names, exceptions and ambiguities.

What have the Age of Reason and the growth of Romanticism to do with modern business? I shall give an (undoubtedly) inadequate but necessary answer later. I shall for now say that business, while aware of its responsibilities, does not so far have a human generational perspective. A paper company may, and often does, plan its stocks of timber forward for fifty years; a water utility may, and often does, plan for supply one hundred years forward; but the human perspective of the corporation remains confined by the canons of its own existence.

The *philosophes* were the first intellectual group in Europe numerous enough to be a *class* of intellectuals. They were an intelligentsia – liberal, skeptical, humane. They were not particularly democratic, but more condescendingly tolerant than most. Their attitude to the Jews was a touchstone of their tolerance: to Montesquieu anti-semitism was a sign of barbarism; Hume condemned the cruelties of their expulsion from England in the 13th century; Lessing in Germany wrote a short play as advocate for them; even Voltaire, who made cynical statements about them, did so because he held Jews to be progenitors of Christianity. As such, he said, when he saw Christians cursing Jews, he saw children beating their fathers. The *philosophes* were prepared to better the fate of the mob, to elevate it, but as pupils rather than as equals. The *philosophes* were, after all, an un-plebeian elite of wits, scholars and gentlemen. In this they did not differ from the founding fathers of the United States, who were also wary of mob, faction and party.

The lights of the French *philosophes* of 18th-century Enlightenment – *Le Siècle des lumières* – were universal Reason, Progress, Nature and Man – above all Reason based on "natural" law.

The encyclopedists were critical universalists, and were by intention – *écrasez l'infâme* – destroyers of inequities. They were deists, not atheists. They believed in a transcendent God, but not a God-in-residence. This meant that the oneness of God and Church, incontestable before, would thenceforth be contestable. It also meant that a sense of selfhood grew beyond the stalls of the confessional, for better or for worse.

But according to d'Alembert, the encyclopaedists were not dedicated to an *esprit de système*, the spirit of a rigid philosophic system, but to an *esprit systématique*, a systematic spirit of enquiry. I interpose: the categories of business are flexible. They are not dogmatic. I too believe that in the shaping of decisions the open-minded approach of an *esprit systématique* is preferable to an *esprit de système*. In the end, too much system means too much rigidity. I believe that the exercise of continuous, educated and energetic judgment is a better business tool than fashionable business theories. A corporation that makes a major decision to invest in new facilities, to merge with or buy another business, to innovate its product line or distribution system, not only immerses itself in only partly charted waters, but also makes the seas it swims in.

The encyclopedists, while (cautiously) exuberant, chose to think concretely. Illustrations of the methods of manufacture and of the applied sciences were part of the *Encyclopédie*, the first volume of which was published in 1751. It was the 18th-century equivalent of the 20th-century Human Genome Project. I find it pleasing, moreover, that the conception of the *Encyclopédie* was a commercial undertaking by André-François Le Breton, a publisher, bookseller and printing-house owner. Initially, it was to be a translation of *Chamber's Cyclopaedia* of 1728; then, with entrepreneurial enthusiasm, an original work, and later a work unequalled in size and scope by any in its day.

The idea of industrial mass-production as a means towards the fulfillment of mankind's dreams began with the *philosophes*, continued into the first half of the 20th century (and was the theme of Chapter 1).

The human soul of religious tradition faded; the human spirit replaced it. So did sensations (sensory perceptions). This presumably had one consequence: because man had a soul and they did not, animals had not officially enjoyed humane consideration. Man was unique. Now animals had something in common with man: awareness of pleasure and of pain – sensations shared by both. This did not stop slaughter; but it has made the slaughterhouse a permanent embarrassment.

Little Foxes: Next Came Political Romanticism

Even while the spirit of Enlightenment suffused France, and variants of it Scotland, England and America, strands of another mentality (already, perhaps unfairly, noted in Kant) began to come to Germany: an anti-materialist, anti-system, anti-rationalist, metaphysically idealist, pro-organic Romanticism; a tempest of the soul rather than Hume's "calm sunshine of the mind;" a counter-Enlightenment.

About half a century later romanticism came to Russia – tinged by hope, Enlightenment, populism, moralism, sentiment, Slavophilia, obscurantism, Dostoyevsky, Tolstoy, lately even Solzhenitzyn. It still persists there – more knitted than woven – despite an iron interlude of more than seventy years. "The Slav world is like a woman who has not yet loved," the Russian Alexander Herzen wrote in 1851. Little has changed this condition since he said it, and Russians are now the last romantics of the Western world. ("Fundamental" Islamic irredentism is conceivably the last romantic movement of the Eastern world.)

John P. Davis noted that in the Middle Ages institutions rather than ideas ruled the world: "The Catholic Church was greater than Catholicism; feudalism was greater than kings or barons." The bottle was, so to speak, more highly valued than the wine. "Modern history, on the contrary, has been distinguished by the growth of ideas rather than of institutions; Protestantism is greater than the Protestant Churches; liberty and equality are greater than parliaments and constitutional kingships."[1]

German romanticism of the 19th century was an illustration of just such a movement from institutions to ideas – and later, unfortunately, back again to repressive institutions – along a fateful path trodden by many. Many of them were academics and sons of Protestant pastors. When the idea came, it came to a country riven into many princedoms; when it departed after National Socialism, it departed from one engulfing state. The wine of romanticism had shaped the bottle of state and nationhood. This is undoubtedly a gross simplification of history; but there is enough truth in it to continue the argument, exemplified by a thoughtful German, writing in 1922 after the experience of World War I.[2] Ernst Troeltsch said that the designation of "Western" had come to be applied to movements in favor of democracy and international understanding. Such movements were then opposed to the specifically "German" way of thought, with its historical and organic character. "Here we touch the core of the contrast." In Western thought "we begin to see, on the one hand, an eternal, rational and divinely ordered system of Order, embracing both morality and law." In the German Romantic Movement of the 19th century, "we begin to see, on the other, individual, living, and perpetually new incarnations of an historically creative Mind." "Those who believe in ... the Equality of man, and a sense of Unity pervading mankind ... cannot but regard the German doctrine as a curious mixture of mysticism and brutality. Those who take the opposite view – who see in history an ever-moving stream – are bound to consider the west-European world of ideas as a world of cold rationalism ..., a world of superficiality and Pharisaism."

The political thought of Germany, he continues, was marked by a curious dualism. On the one hand, Romanticism and lofty idealism. On the other, a realism which went to the verge of cynicism and of utter indifference to all ideals and all morality. "But what you will see above all," he says in a celebrated statement, "is an inclination ... to brutalize romance, and to romanticize cynicism." (Though celebrated, the statement is celebrated by few.)

The problem was the injection of the "spirit of nationhood" into the debate. It transformed liberal nationalism into romantic nationalism. The fatal sequence – I shall be brief, rough, and probably unfair – went like this:

Every individual is his own Prometheus. He is free to pit his will against the gods of chilly rationality. Reason, Luther had earlier said, "is the greatest enemy of faith." Virtue, Kant had said, is "a compulsion according to a principle of *inner* freedom." "My will rules fate" Schleiermacher had said in 1800.

The prescription to oppose was also a cultural and literary movement, a Storm and Thrust, a *Sturm und Drang*, a deep romantic longing. It expanded from literature to invade interpretations of history and the theory of the law. Following Savigny (1779–1861), one of the legal protagonists of the Romantic movement in Germany, the *Volksgeist* was to be "the starting-point of a deeper and profounder theory of society."[3]

Towards the middle of the 19th century, "faith," "will," and "inner freedom" looked romantically at man, found him too weak a vessel, and replaced him with the titanic will of Man-as-Hero. It is one of the minor accidents of history that Thomas Carlyle found himself very short of money in 1840: "If dire famine drive me" onto the "bayonets of Necessity," he wrote to his brother and to Emerson, he would have to lecture. Famine did, and so he lectured.

He searched for a subject. In the end, he chose critical eulogies of real and mythical persons – among them the Nordic god Odin, Mohammed, Dante and Shakespeare – and called the series of six lectures *On Heroes and the Heroic in History*. They economized on facts, but were brilliant (historically) romantic evocations. Nietzsche read them, and it may be a coincidence that Nietzsche's surrogate for God and Christianity, the Superman, Overman, *Übermensch* with a "will to power," was an imaginative mutant of Carlyle's Hero. Nietzsche cannot be blamed for the use Hitler made of him. Still, the Nazis, viciously, made an adaptive mutation of Romanticism.

Marx made another. Marx found his hero, now collective, in the "proletariat," a class which as a class has vanished. (Its supposed enemy, the class of capitalistic business people, classlessly survives.)

The "romantic" movement, which now embraced a new reading of history and the law, became a national and a nationalist movement – an Existentialism of the Whole Nation, in a way. It sought to be distinctive, group-minded, associative, anti-international and anti-cosmopolitan. It differentiated itself from foreigners, strangers, "others." It fostered opposition to them, but disliked opposition to itself. It began to institutionalize these ideas so that the state became the undoubted master-guardian of the *Volksgeist*. Finally, unimpugnably, the state *was* the *Volksgeist* made flesh. It culminated in Hitler.

On the other hand, in this half-century, Germans and Japanese, whose mentality is associative, have (so far) done better in industry than weakly associative peoples like Arabs, Malays, Argentinians and the English.

Little Foxes: Nationalism Followed – no Friend of Business

Nor was the defeat of Hitler the end of existential Romanticism. Nationalism persists, unhealed and festering, as a primitive romanticism of wounded nations. Foreign oppression partly accounts for it, but oppression calls for liberty, which is not the same as nationhood. When a degree of freedom came to the peoples of the former Soviet empire, its fragmentation into separate nations brought no notable advancement of their liberties to some of them. Nationalism has many economic causes, but it is non-economic as a sentiment. It fits badly into the careful ways of business and its canny weighing of advantage. It seems to issue from a moody, invisible ventriloquist whose voice is echoed by the belly sentiments of a thousand unforgiving human dummies.

Nationalism is a reduced definition of man's common humanity. It is a condition in which a narrow difference is seen as the only difference that matters. It often arises from a sense of being slighted, which may be real or imagined (mostly ima-gined). The slight festers and separates Slovaks from Czechs; Ukrainians from Russians; Croats from Serbs. Nationalism comes to harbor the curiously mistaken notion that being toge-ther is achieving. It hopes that, somehow, separateness may by itself be a fulfillment, and that even a tiny sovereignty will ensure an international parity of esteem. But, as Elie Kedourie has pointed out, national self-determination has proved to be more often a principle of disorder than of order in international life.[4] I am far from wanting to deny a homeland to a nation; but I resist the notion that a homeland can be gained by the excision of neighbors.

Nationalism does not become rebellious at a time when answers are available; it becomes rebellious at a time when only questions are available. Amid the passion of nationalist fervor a people asks Who are our friends? and gives the wrong answer; it asks Who are our enemies? and again gives the wrong answer.

Despite its protestations, nationalism has deeper roots in domestic equality than in domestic liberty. In vain; because an assault by native wolves usually follows the expulsion of foreign hyenas. (It is, incidentally, not difficult to spot a nationalist: not only does he dislike foreigners – he does not like his own people much either.)

The results of national irredentism only show after it has taken place; the outcome disappoints, and new Phoenix-nations rise with singed pinions. When nationalism ultimately decides to make use of the products of other cultures, it is, for many years, too late to be of any use.

There are few preventive answers to nationalism. Wealth sometimes helps. Trade sometimes helps. But neither education nor religion guarantee tolerance and toleration. Late 19th-century Central European education, inspired by the Jahns and Fichtes of the day, made things worse. So do some modern religious fundamentalisms – among Christians, Muslims and Jews.

Nationalism is a peculiar form of ignorance in that, while all the means towards an understanding and enjoyment of other cultures now exist, no use is made of them. Rather than trouble to learn something from their neighbors, nationalists only entrench the inbred acquaintance of themselves more deeply. This inner "knowledge" of themselves includes false readings of history and is stuffed full of home-made myths and fictions. One of these fictions is that the command of national "destiny" may override the demands of conscience.

Small states are founded based upon such myths and fictions. But myths and fictions make inbred rather than expansive nations. They seek sovereignty; but being small, they can only achieve dependency on foreign business. Nationalists fight for land as though this were the only resource of value. Theirs is a lapse back into the medieval warrior's view that commerce, art, peace and industry are nothing, and land is everything.

The persistence of extreme nationalism, nativism, tribalism, chauvinism and xenophobia shows how useless is a "global age of information" when signals are bounced off the skin instead of settling in as knowledge. There will be a long wait before the muses sing again after the guns have cooled.

Pluralism Dominates the West

Two thousand years ago no European people lived where it now lives, had been what it is now, had the gods it now has, or spoke the language it now speaks. Seen from this perspective, modern nationalism measures history with coffee spoons and takes pride in origins that are largely spurious and recent. The fury of nationalism sounds strange to the metropolitan, historical, civilized and Western ear, with – here I egregiously idealize the average Western citizen – his more inward love of country, his more tolerant patriotism, his greater law-abidingness, his respectful pluralism and more judicious sense of his nation's past.

Americans have a sense more of continentality than of nationality. Many things shaped them; foremost amongst these was that almost no trace of Europe's feudalist past entered their lives and laws. For Americans, their nationality is a political and moral concept. In a sense, they, like the Jews, are a nomocracy. The Jews found essence in a Holy Writ; Americans find it in the treasured texts of the preamble to the Declaration of Independence, the Constitution, the Bill of Rights and the Gettysburg Address. These, rather than ethnic uniformity, shaped them. What inspires Americans is not the format of their constitution but its poetry. What shaped them even more was a curious, Calvinistic alliance between moralism and acquisitiveness, which they regarded as consistent rather than contradictory values. This combination has, by transference, also molded business in the Western world since World War II. Americans are not as individualistic when at work as is often believed. The influx of many Germans in and before the 19th century has left its mark on organization, cooperation and on the attitude towards collective effort.

Russians have a strong sense of identity. But it is spongy: history has not yet offered them an opportunity to fuse character and civilization into a unity. Not institutions or constitutions – of which they have so far had none of fairness or meaning – but their literature, liturgy and music are the patrimony of Russian culture. These are in the keeping of the Russian Middle Class – of which, unfortunately, there are two kinds. One is the traditional Russian "intelligentsia," composed of professionals and academics. They are intellectuals in the European mold, whose culture is grounded in the European tradition. The other is also of the middle, but consists of former *"apparatchiks,"* former communist party functionaries in the higher reaches of government and industry, who were on the list of the named, the ranked and numbered *"nomenklatura,"* and who are accustomed to power and economic privilege. So far, they still retain possession of many of their privileges and much of their power. They are in Adam Smith's category of managers, technocrats, bureaucrats and "merchants who contrive a conspiracy against the public wherever they meet." A fusion of these two middle classes has not yet been accomplished in some countries of the former Soviet Union, including Russia itself.

The English have a greater sense of identity than of nationality. Their patriotism, normally inward, wavers between sentimentality and jingoism, between solidarity in crises and disjunction normally. Outbreaks of jingoism today are rough and grating because England has not bred traditional forms of patriotic expression. In one of his essays G.K. Chesterton was pithy: "Oh what a happy place England would be to live in if only one did not love it." Perhaps the English hardly trouble to think of themselves as a nation because they find it easier to think of themselves as a species. It works both ways: non-English peoples, when they consider mankind in general, can hardly imagine it as English. The English cannot see themselves as Americans; but are surprised to find that Americans are un-English. They can live with incongruity: as a court of law, for example, the House of Lords was (until a few decades ago) bound by its own past decisions; the House of Commons, on the contrary, cannot bind future parliaments. Their tolerance of incongruity notwithstanding, the English will, together with the rest of Britain, in the end join the European Union fully because they have made the choice of poverty too often in the past.

The Germans' sense of national identity is strong but still unsettled; and their sense of nationality and identity are conflated: who shall be German is still (as I write) more largely determined by "blood" origins than by residence or domicile. Being young as a unified country, there is much regionalism about, typified by the Bavarian who, in World War II, vilified Winston Churchill as "that Prussian swine."

For the French and Québecois, linguistic and cultural identity coincides with nationhood – in the sense that Frenchness is both nationality and membership of a great but solitary linguistic civilization. It may almost be that the French, as well they ought, are more fascinated by their civilization (Michelet's

"France is a religion") than by their nationality. In business, France has a curious leadership system of elites to act for the public good of the corporation and the nation, which is in direct line of descent from the Enlightenment's belief in the "best" of men and the best in man.

On the other hand, Joubert's statement that the French are "moved only by greed" is as feebly justified as the statement that the English are "a nation of shopkeepers." In both cases it might have been better for their national economies had these statements been true.

Long after Mazzini and Garibaldi, Italians are still fonder of region than nation – a legacy, perhaps, of the rich history of their city cultures and of the fact that standard Italian is still only the language of culture and government – comprehensible but not native to most Italians.

Pluralism does not go with nationalism but goes with business. Romanticism goes with nationalism but does not go with business. In short, nationalism does not go with business (unless protectionism now, and the mercantilism, balance-of-trade-ism and cameralism of the 17th and 18th centuries, are counted as abandoned forms of it). Trade and international investment disaffirm nationalism in the West. Love-of-country and nationalism are no longer synonymous terms. They have become separate concepts, and are often each other's enemy. It is at any rate certain that the transnationalism of business has done more for world wealth and welfare in the second half of this century than all the many little nationalisms from Woodrow Wilson onward.

While every culture and nation has its own particular conventions of honest behavior, business has one enveloping set of standards of what constitutes commercial, fiduciary and financial *dis*honesty. These standards are high, and they homogenize the standards of the world. The Japanese playwright Masakazu Yamazaki (*Foreign Affairs*, July 1996) agrees that such

Western standards arch over distinct national civilizations and overlay them.

Little Foxes: National Cultures versus Global Capitalism

To believe that capitalism is wholly imperfectible would be a prior admission of defeat. On the other hand, few would argue that capitalism as it stands is perfect (other than ageing Thatcher–Reagan 1980s zealots). The prevailing view is that capitalism is basically fit and fine, but does need, and will need, continuous tuning here and there.

Given that nationalism in the West is a weaker force than business transnationalism, does it matter that differences in national mentalities remain? Does capitalism have to be uniform to be effective?

"The future is out there; it cannot be made" is a quick-profit mentality. It is common in the United Kingdom and is one of the reasons why the UK has a highly reactive City, accomplished asset strippers, but much deficient industry. British finance understands money well as a commodity; but it does not always think it necessary to understand the intimate nexus between work and money.

"The future is not out there; it must be made" is the personal view of most Americans, though not of American business leaders under pressure. It is firmly the German view, the Japanese view, and, with a little deference to customary skepticism, the view of France's business leaders. Italian industrialists have not yet decided the question, but Italian furniture and fashion designers work on the assumption that the future can be made.

In essence, capitalism is a culturally and morally neutral sorting mechanism, a means of allocating scarcities and giving them a price. In so doing it creates modes of organization and production, modes of life, and wealth. Not its essence but its modes and fruits butt up against the values, habits and cultures of nations. This does not matter when capitalism and culture are compatible, as by and large they are in the United States. It *does* matter when they are not. When they are not compatible, capitalism generally wins in time because it creates wealth while "culture" does not. This process is now being obviously demonstrated in Russia.

Culture sometimes furthers capitalism. After World War II, Japan was greatly helped by a "duty" culture – the obligation citizens feel towards the fatherhood of their employer and the cousinship of fellow employees. Japan's culture, unlike India's, also had a tradition of standard measurements, *tatami* mats and window modules, which made industrial precision familiar to it from the start. Does it therefore matter that Japanese civilization still requires an inefficient but cozy and stable domestic distribution system which is as characteristic of its culture as efficient industries? The system will of course be changed when the many static tiers of distribution begin to seriously impair Japan's wealth.

The social wave of political humanitarianism after World War II altered the nature of Western capitalism (as did the trends described in Chapter 1). So did a third factor – a humanistic trend – which arbitrates between cultures and capitalism: a global "general will" towards peace, security, free trade and coexistence exemplified by the spirit which sustains the United Nations and other global institutions.

But, as we have seen, culture is grandeur. In the West it is national pride and not national hatreds; and as such a matter worth preserving.

Business Relationships: Pluralism versus Nationalism

No barriers, save one, divide business and liberal democracy. That barrier is the conflict between "success" and "conviction."

Jane Jacobs's robust *Systems of Survival*[5] fruitfully divides attitudes into those of "traders" (which partly overlaps my "ethos of success"); and "guardians" (which partly overlaps my "ethos of conviction").

The "trader's" code, she says, is contractual and thrifty, shunning force; the "guardian's" code is forceful and munificent, shunning trade. "Trading" is the province of commerce. "Guardianship" is the province of the state and uncommercial occupations: of bureaucracies, of armies and of landed classes. Status, "honor" and valor mark the guardian's code; caution, contracts and honorable dealing mark the trader's.

The business mind is not naturally inclined to passionate love of competition. Meekness is not a business value either. Monopoly is lovely: it is more comfortable by far to have the market to oneself. But failing all else, competition is imposed on business by the state as "guardian." Yet without competition – Adam Smith was right – the business system would be predatory. Therefore the "trader" and the "guardian," though not in natural alliance, depend on one another. "Conviction" needs success, and "success" needs conviction. Without the "ennobling functions" of the state (George Wills's phrase) and without the common conscience of its parliaments, citizens and churches, the trader could not himself acquire a claim to a nobility of calling. Nor could business make level playing fields unaided by the "guardian's" will and power.

"Conviction" and "success" often have opposing interests. "Conviction" may say that profit is a great evil and must be abolished. "Success" may say that profit is a great virtue which will solve the problems of the world. And yet "guardians" and their convictions, and "traders" and their desire for success, are beginning to converge. "Traders" are now involved in forms of guardianship; while governments, traditionally guardians, try to calculate the ratio of cost to success. Governments now commercialize; to a lesser extent, "traders" with a public conscience impinge on spheres of public interest. Alongside these, more public interest organizations, charities and foundations exist which apply the criteria of success and effectiveness to the criteria of conviction and principle. Operationally, they are capitalists without a profit motive.

Conclusion and Summary

Seen as a whole, business is the most embracing institution of the modern world. But no single corporation is a representative institution of society. No single corporation has much more at heart than its own problems and, at best, the problems of its immediate, identifiable stakeholders. To find a broader perspective business must join with other institutions of society in what is bound to be a humanist mixed economy. The mix will not only be an economic requirement in the future, but a requirement of civilized society.

6

Corporations: The Poacher Become Gamekeeper

Corporations are complex adaptive systems. They wind their course between the laws of property and the proprieties of life. In so doing they transform themselves, the licenses of property, and everyone's lives.

Until the early 20th century corporations had legal form without a social function. By 1955, an acute American observer was able to say that they had become dominant social, legal, economic and political institutions. He warned that if corporate managers based their tenure on power and not on reason, the end would be disaster, which might be the consequence not of creeping socialism but of galloping capitalism.[1]

Corporations have three foundations: limited liability; the general right of incorporation; freedom and its transforming consequence: social responsibility.

This chapter looks at these and at the respective rights of four claimants: the corporation itself, its shareholders, its stakeholders, and society.

Corporations: The Poacher Become Gamekeeper

Frankenstein, or the Making of Artificial Persons

Limited liability was a revolutionary first principle. It transformed commercial action by a person or groups of persons into
action by a single corporate person. No previous invention of
society had created such a collective individual, and no previous
legal invention has had such far-reaching consequences.

Limited liability came to the laws of England in the 15th
century when a court ruled that that which is owed by or to the
whole is not owed by or to its members separately.

The second and allied principle, incorporation, came in
parts: at the end of the 16th century by special royal charters for
corporations; in the 19th century by general law. The difference
is marked. A charter was *concessionary*: the king granted or
conceded monopoly to one corporation to take out and bring in
defined goods in and out of defined territories. But incorporation
by general law was to be an *inherent* right of association. It
extinguished the right to monopoly.

The general right to found a corporation did not arise from
any glow of law-givers' magnanimity. It arose because chartered
corporations had made excessive use of the privileges of
monopoly. And so parliaments allowed free incorporation by
statute; this continued to permit limited liability but no longer

granted unique privilege. It happened in New York in the 1820s, in the 1840s in Britain, in the 1860s and 1870s in France and Germany. Indeed, some states of the USA prohibit incorporation by specific charter.

At first glance the concept of a general right of incorporation is curious. It holds that the continuous conflict of competition brings harmonious balance. Harmony through conflict is not, fortunately, an entirely wrong-headed concept. With it goes the parallel belief that the power of some aggregations is largely offset by the power of other aggregations, and that therefore society need only deal with uncancelled remainders. In a sense, popular democracy is based on the similar principle that when a party obtains a majority, the uncancelled surplus of votes permits it to govern for a term.

One might suppose that a society based on sustained agreement is preferable to a society based on continuous tension. But it is troubling that in societies which rely on "social harmony" – like Japan, Singapore and Indonesia – such harmony is frequently impressed on the people by social or political sanctions. All too often the outward harmony of a nation is nothing but the cultural colonization of a dependent majority by an established and powerful minority. Harmony undoubtedly exists as an ideal and (partial) reality; but if one asks on whose terms the harmony is based, one finds it to be an unwanted and unanswered question.

The Poachers' Charter

From the late 16th and in the 17th century many circumstances led to the emergence of large chartered corporations, which were experiments in privatization that rotted soon, did not fulfill their promise, were inefficient, and ultimately failed. Their emergence was due (not necessarily in order of importance or chronology) to the growth of foreign trade; the presence of a class of moneyed investors of whom the English part were often called adventurers or merchant adventurers; the art of navigation; the availability of larger ships; the fear of pirates, buccaneers, privateers or freebooters, and hence the need for convoys; the business of insurance, so that the Amsterdam Insurance Company, for example, maintained a fleet of sixty men-of-war to escort the vessels it had insured; the popularity of tropical produce such as cotton, spices, tea, coffee and cane sugar; the demand for the carriage of slaves to work plantations and sugar mills; mercantilism (the theory that national wealth is not so much what a nation can produce through work and skills than the amount of treasure in the coffers of its kings and merchants) with its love of silver and gold bullion, and ships to carry soldiers for the necessary work of rapine and butchery to get it; royal rivalry conjoined with mercantilism by the Portuguese, the Spanish, the Dutch, the French, the English, and even for a short time the Swedish; the joy of kings and their merchants at the conquest of colonial possessions; the flight of religious minorities to pastures free of persecution though not free of other dangers; and once all this had started, the need to maintain and protect colonial acquisitions and monopolies.

Many of the chartered corporations genuinely had things to sell and things to buy; but some were (c)argonauts setting sail to capture golden fleeces from imagined mutton. There was indeed one often-mentioned scheme in England which advertised itself to potential investors as "an undertaking of Great Advantage, but nobody to know what it is." Corruption and "insider dealing" were endemic: Winston Churchill's *History of the English-Speaking Peoples* records that in the collapse, in 1720, of the chartered South Sea Company (the "South Sea Bubble") 462 members of the lower house of Parliament (a majority of the House of Commons) and 122 members of the upper (House of Lords) were implicated as "insiders."

One of the results of the commercial opportunities created by these activities was a shift of the horizons of commerce from Europe's seas to the world's oceans. Another was the migration of Europeans. There were some exceptions: not commerce but chains caused migration to Australia; not opportunity but fetters caused the migration of African slaves to the West Indies and America. On the other hand, in places where local labor was tractable and cheap, as in the islands of Indonesia, imported slaves were not required.

On the last day of the 17th century, December 31st 1600, Elizabeth I of England granted a corporate charter to "certain adventurers," to be called "The Governor and Company of Merchants of London Trading into the East Indies" or East India Company. It was to become the greatest of many chartered joint-stock corporations. The charter assigned to the company "the whole, entire and only trade" to the East Indies, to the exclusion of any others except by license from the Company and under its laws. The Company was also empowered to enforce its monopoly by fines on offenders and by their imprisonment.

The East Indies charter was similar to many granted by several nations before and after the turn of the 17th century. Besides the East India Company, England had chartered the Merchant Adventurers, the Muscovy (or Russian) Company, the Levant Company, the Royal African Company, the Hudson's Bay Company, the South Sea Company, and others to trade into France, Turkey and Spain. Charters were granted for the commercial advancement of Virginia, Massachusetts and Pennsylvania. Spain and Portugal maintained their conquests as royal monopolies rather than entrust them to chartered companies. But France, too, established an East India Company and a Company of the East Indies. The Dutch had their Dutch West India Company, Dutch East India Company and Dutch East Indies Company. Though historically significant, most were unprofitable at the time.

It is well-known that the Dutch West India Company bought Manhattan from the native Indians for 60 guilders (35 in present US$) in 1626, named it New Amsterdam, granted only five manorial privileges along the Hudson river to Dutch "patroons" (substantial agricultural patrons) in "New Netherland," and lost what became New York to the English some forty years later. Considering subsequent losses and write-offs, it may well be that 60 guilders had been too high a price to pay. Few Dutch farmers settled the land under the Dutch regime. Most of them, together with farmers of other nationalities who had become Dutch in language and culture (including some Poles) settled New Jersey and Southern New York after the surrender to the English and continued to farm and build steep gambrel-roofed stone houses there in the Dutch style until the 1840s. I mention this because I lived and had my business in one of them for several years.

Next to the English East India Company, the most prosperous was the chartered Dutch East India Company. Its chief conquest was Java and other parts of what has since become Indonesia. Investment in the Company was democratically open to Europeans but autocratically closed to Javans. With little kindness, it enforced a hugely profitable monopoly on native clove and pepper, and later on coffee. It paid high dividends and survived until the end of the 18th century when the Dutch government terminated its charter because it had become bloated and corrupt.

But the history of chartered corporations runs deep, and has not ceased entirely. In the 1980s, Britain and France decided that a Channel Tunnel between them should finally be built – a project first mooted a century or so ago. Yet Britain did not want to spend public money to finance it. Private and corporate investors were found, and the Eurotunnel company was formed. In return for its risk the Company asked for and received from France and Britain its prospectively greatest asset: the privilege of a sole right until the year 2020, conditionally renewable until the middle of the coming century, to build and operate the present and all future channel tunnels. It was a "concession" that unquestionably has in it some of the hallmarks of the chartered company of centuries ago.

Nor has all monopoly ceased. The diamond industry of South Africa and the Soviet Union markets most gem and industrial diamonds of the world through London, and has done so for many years. No anti-trust law – Sherman or other – has as yet defeated it.

i.e 2050

Nations as Poachers: Mercantilism

But this chapter is about the nature of corporations rather than their history. I mention the East India Company below not to recount its story, but because it was an "organization around which centred most of the economic controversies of the seventeenth century."[2]

One of these was mercantilism and its fear of loss of bullion. The East India Company was often accused, by Daniel Defoe for example, of taking more gold out of the country than it brought in. The Company refuted the charge: it claimed that it had brought more precious cargo from India and China than England herself needed, the surplus having been sold to other countries for much gold. It thus claimed that it had brought more money into the Kingdom than it had taken out of it. Much of the time the refutation was correct. Yet because men, in Keynes's words, are often "slaves of some defunct economists," and because the mercantilists of the day were not only such slaves but also the official "madmen in authority," the Company could never scuttle the charge completely.

What the soil – indestructible and green – had been to the minds of feudal lords and countrymen in the Middle Ages, gold – indestructible and yellow – was to the minds of urban merchants and mercantilists: the ultimate resource. Not until the middle of the 18th century, when David Hume and Adam Smith mounted their assaults on mercantilism was it gradually abandoned in favour of free trade and *laissez faire*. In essence, Hume and Smith proclaimed that work-makes-wealth-makes-money, and not that money-makes-wealth-makes-work. This practice (omitting the sweat of their own work, of course) was already being used pragmatically by the stockholders of the East India Company, regardless of the doctrine of the day. Note incidentally, that *money-makes-wealth-makes-work* is still a core belief of European and American "trickle-down" conservatives, and that *work-makes-wealth-makes-money* is still a core belief of European and American non-conservatives, but also, notably, of Japanese conservatives.

In any case, the mercantilist credo could not make sense of credit. Credit is not minted money, but it is not not money either. If what-I-owe-you was offset in reasonable time by what-you-owe-me, no coin changed hands though something had happened. Credit was amply used by all who were involved in trade. Daniel Defoe, writing in 1725/6, estimated that two thirds of the trade of England was conducted on credit – an example of the way in which low practice makes nonsense of high dogma.

Adam Smith called mercantilism the "mercantile system." If it was a system, it was not known as such by those who applied it. Rather, it was the combative and "natural" way in which nations then behaved: commerce was a tool of the state's interests. The competition of other states was, if necessary, a *casus belli*, a sufficient cause for war against them. Chartered companies were not nationalized entities by ownership, but they were national entities by the interests of the state – which is why portions of the sovereignty of the state as master were granted to its servant companies by way of sovereign monopoly. Needless to say, the servant, being in search of money more than patriotism, was often disobedient; and needless to say, the servants of these servants were often corrupt.

As Lipson tells it, the history of the East India Company was "primarily the history of a mercantile body which grew into a sovereign power. In the seventeenth century it had received privileges at the hand of native [Indian] princes: in the following century it conferred them."[3] But in the 19th century, 273 years after receiving its first charter, it ceased to be. The British Crown retook full and undiluted empire over India, only to surrender it, in 1947, to a small man with five hundred million voices.

Finally, the East India Company and its like was a forerunner of the modern publicly quoted corporation limited as to shares. This development, though it may sound a little technical, was immensely important: it was important because stock exchanges have become most people's chief investment mechanism; and important because it demonstrates that the logic of money generally prevails over political theory.

More Freedom for Corporations than for Individuals

After the first two principles – limited liability, and incorporation by general right – came the third: freedom, and its late 20th-century transforming consequence, social responsibility.

The principle of liberty for corporations did not arise before the idea of liberty for the individual had been pushed to the foreground by the Enlightenment of the late 18th century. It may not have occured to Voltaire, Diderot, d'Alembert and Holbach, to Hume and Adam Smith, to Kant and Lessing, to Franklin and Jefferson, that it would bring more liberty to the corporation than to the individual.

According to John Davis,[4] only when individual rights and obligations "became plain to the eye of the English law" was it able to see corporate rights in clear relief. Corporations had until then been "viewed not so much as divisions of society as associations of individuals." It was on the assumption that private rights for individuals were inherent by "the law of nature" that the corporations could, by means of a legal fiction (a "legal exaltation") be seen as a sort of extended persons equally endowed with private rights – as "enlarged individuals, not reduced societies." Yet at the end of his important book on corporations John Davis complains, even one hundred years ago, that they had grown to the point at which the citizen discovered "that citizenship in his country has been largely metamorphosed into membership in corporations, and patriotism into fidelity to them."

As to the meaning of "artificial": Yes, corporations are born by legal pronouncement; and No, they cannot be killed by hanging or by shooting. But though in this sense artificial, nothing is more visible, real and corporeal than these "lesser commonwealths." The constant metamorphosis of the world is, in great measure, the result of their ambitions.

The Gamekeeper's Duties

While the wealth of corporations is great, it is relatively less great than it was at the beginning of this century. Since then, the capital of private persons has grown more rapidly than that of corporations, and private ownership of houses, cars, furniture, works of art, savings, life insurances and annuities, and so on, has an asset value which corporations can hardly match. Add to private assets the immensely increased balance-sheet value of government installations (estimated, because governments do not issue balance sheets and are careless of depreciation accounting) – roads, harbors, infrastructures of all kinds, military ordnance and ships, meteorology, schools, universities, public buildings, public parks, and so on – and the wealth of corporations has diminished in relative terms. Nevertheless, corporations still preponderate in other ways because their wealth is by its nature concentrated and is applied with single-mindedness.

Corporations, notwithstanding that they are created as *personae fictae* (imaginary, legal, artificial, juridical, or fictitious persons) are *personae*, persons; and are therefore residents or citizens under the law. That some corporations are citizens of the world rather than citizens of one state does not affect the argument. It being the duty of residents and citizens to be neighborly, it is the duty of corporations also to be neighborly. Capital is "clothed with a public trust."

This is not a newly minted special obligation particular to corporations, but an ancient obligation in all civilizations. Maine, in "Ancient Law," even contended that a corporation may be considered not so much a legal person as a legal family.[5] If so, then a sense of familial obligations may be all the more expected from it. Many of its employees may not be responsible for a corporation's actions and may therefore be "dead in law," but it is proper to assume that they are alive as claimants.

And what, in moderation, goes for employees, goes for communities; what goes for communities, goes for future generations; what goes for the clean air about the corporation, goes for the clean air that keeps the world's population healthy.

What is curious is not that these obligations exist, but that they were for so long either neglected, or ignored, or thought not to exist. True, more than is the case for private persons, "to touch the corporation is to touch much else."[6] But precisely because it touches much else, it cannot go untouched itself, any more than can a private citizen remain untouched by citizenly duty.

In the United States, corporations, like private persons, enjoy the protection of their "life, liberty and property" under the Fourteenth Amendment to the Constitution. But where there are overt rights there are usually implied duties. Indeed, "if the controlling management of the big dispersedly owned corporations adopted the role of arbiter among stockholders, workers, and consumers the courts might accept such a role."[7] At heart is the general question whether the corporation is only a productive unit, or also a moral unit. France, for example, speaks of the corporation as having a *personnalité morale,* a moral personality. And insofar as they transform society, corporations owe a duty to it.

The corporation is not intended to be sublime; indeed it would be harmful if it tried. It needs no exalted destinations. In 1961, two respected American authors[8] could say that it is now the lot of the economic organization, given its power and persuasiveness in the lives of all of us, not to seek so much to form new values as to be conscientious and rational in the application, in new circumstances, of those that have been preached and taught and legislated in the United States for the last three hundred years. Yet thirty years later, who can say that what was "conscientious and rational application" then is sufficiently conscientious and rational today? The corporation was once subject to legal or political attack for exceeding its statutory purposes, as was the East India Company; now, when attacked, it is more often for offending against public, social, or moral interests and ideas.

The German jurist Gierke (1841–1921) regarded the corporation as a living unity which has a will and can turn will into deed. More soberly, an opposing English judgment held that a corporation is a fiction recognized by law, "created and existing only for the convenient transaction of business." Neither definition covers the social and political consequences of a corporation's "convenient transactions," or of obligations arising from such consequences.

Corporations are a critical juncture: having been devised as commercial entities, they have in addition become sociological entities. In 1897 John Davis wrote that the corporation question was "primarily a question of social form and only secondarily one of social function."[9] The secondary function now ranks equally with the primary function. Most acts of legislation and regulation are more concerned, excessively at times, to make corporations societally acceptable than to make them efficient.

Social meanings – right or wrong – are ascribed to many of the acts of corporations. As a result, there is confusion of who does what for whom, with what authority this is done and what is a proper use of corporate power and responsibility. Therefore, a narrow description may be made of the respective roles of those who affect, and are affected by, corporate actions:

Management. In Roman terminology but with sufficient modern meaning, the corporation and its management has *quiritary* rights and duties. That is to say that it has legal rights and obligations (which are distinct from the equitable rights of shareholders and the beneficial rights of stakeholders). Ultimately, its duties are fiduciary: they are to do what is best for the corporation itself as an operating entity, and to remain unswayed by harmful pressures. These pressures may be external: pressures by some for hasty profits, by others for wages and salaries beyond the bounds of realism. Or they may be internal: excessive self-awards by top management, and empire-building for the sake of empire.

Shareholders have *equitable* rights, that is, proprietary rights because they are "owners." This on the face of it seems right, except for transformations in the nature of ownership. Old-fashioned "ownership" rights reemerge almost fully when the corporation is floundering, sinking, or drowning (see Chapter 10). At other times, the meaning of ownership is reduced to the buying and selling of shares for investment or speculative gain – some of it by individuals, most of it by other corporations or by pension and insurance funds.

Stockholders and shareholders are no longer considered, even by some courts, as sole beneficiaries of the corporations' activities. In a 1954 test case,[10] the Superior Court of New Jersey upheld a large gift to Princeton University. It proclaimed that "what promotes the general good inescapably enhances the corporation weal." It held that giving is within the "incidental powers" of corporations.

Stakeholders. The corporation's employees, (sometimes) its unfunded pensioners, charities, the surrounding community, and others, have *bonitary* rights, that is, beneficial rights – claims which are imperfectly defined, which overlap proprietary rights, but which seem nevertheless to have turned into *prima facie* rights. Most of these are founded on a new perception of "natural" rights rather than on legislation. The claim to them is based on a rising requirement by society for corporations to become humanist entities. The idea of "stakeholding" as a right has become prominent in political debate, especially in the United Kingdom where it seems to be a movement to make state humanitarianism partly private and corporate humanism partly public. As such, the notion of "stakeholding" begins (as yet a little romantically) to buttress the claims of society.

Society, the fourth claimant, also asserts its minimum "natural" rights of public benefit, of environmental wholesomeness, and more. This, too, is one of society's increasingly forceful requirements for a more humanistic and neighborly face for business – a spiking of the "ethos of success" with elements of the "ethos of conviction."

But clearly this entire mix of rights, claims and partial satisfactions is still incompletely settled, and is sometimes even self-contradictory. The capitalist Proteus will remain, but the mix will change its forms, its functions and its purposes. And if the mix is thus perceived as only a temporary settlement, then with good reason: for that is what it is – a working settlement *pro tem*.

Summary and Conclusion

Beyond a point, growth means qualitative transformation. Though they have had ancient precursors, in the last one hundred years or so corporations have grown from marginal economic vehicles for private profit to complex and dominating sectors of society with an immense dynamic of enterprise, investment, productivity, invention and singleness of purpose.

The corporation's responsibilities to its shareholders have not changed. But domains of irresponsibility have been reduced and are reducing. Stakeholders – employees and community – have been given beneficial rights; environment now impinges on the conduct of operations; society now asserts its expectations and its prohibitions. Business has become an inseparable part of the structure of nations. Those ideologues, including heads of state, who propounded the simple-minded ideology of untrammelled enterprise not long ago, are now irrelevant. Realism is assuredly a virtue in the practice of management, but realism includes regard for the souls of neighbors. The difficulty is, of course, that "soul" is an expense.

7

The Profit of Maximal Profit

*There is, first, a fundamental discordance between the heart of business
and the heart of governance. A nation's government must, almost by
definition, be patriotic. Even when it is in favor of, say, free trade,
government must invoke the national interest to justify it. Business, on
the other hand, is not at all designed for patriotism. The duty of management is to maximize the return to shareholders and satisfactions to
stakeholders. Its first duty is to survive and be profitable – at home or
abroad. In times of peace, therefore, patriotism is a luxury.*

*Next, there is discordance between degrees of predatoriness and
degrees of civility within the firm. Depending on conduct this too may
lead to regulation and to conflict with civil governance.*

*There is, last, a basic misinterpretation about the nature and
purpose of profits. Stock exchanges and financial markets on the one
hand, industries and major service businesses on the other, have*

different criteria and time perspective. Yet non-financial businesses in the USA and Britain are forced to use the shortened horizons of the money markets. A fundamental discordance exists when one – industry – wants to see profits in their proper role as offsets to future costs and as the funding of continuance, while the other – banks and financial markets – see variously packaged money as directly margin-earning goods without the intermediacy of product.

The Profit of Maximal Profit .

Patriotism is Unprofitable

"Merchants," said Thomas Jefferson, "have no country." A
corporation is not unpatriotic by sentimental inclination but by
the nature of business. To meet its profit targets and obligations
to stockholders it must look to lawful gain wherever this may be
found – as one of the appropriate confirmations that it is doing
its proper job across state borders and in distant continents. This
has little to do with the loyalties, private sentiments and patri-
otisms of its management and employees. Prudence merely
requires that managements which cast off the chains of one
country do not fall into the shackles of another.

Governments are manifestly obliged to be patriotic by the
nature of their popular constituency. But there is no legal or
practical obligation on corporations to be patriotic. (There is an
obligation to pay taxes. But paying taxes is part of normal conduct, not of patriotic duty.) Hence occasional conflict between
business and government is inherent in the market system. This
explains why what is considered good for General Motors is not
always considered good for the United States of America.

But it is the case that in the United States in the Reagan and
Bush years, and in Great Britain in the Thatcher years, governments so persuaded themselves that the market system was a
patriotic as well as a national economic model that they ignored

the tensions between them. It then became apparent that a monetary policy of high interest rates, while salutary for some economic purposes, destroyed industrial competitiveness and investment and, consequently, the competitiveness of exports.

At the time, the governments of the United States and the United Kingdom were enchanted (and enchained) by the idea of markets. They believed them to be great engines of creation, which they are; and only of creation, which they are not. They forgot that, when policy so indicates, markets are also engines of destruction. A wave of de-industrialization came, but for years only a sluggish wave of re-industrialization followed. They were slow to learn that fiscal and industrial policy has to stand squarely alongside money.

It is another of the paradoxes of the profit motive that corporations are apatriotic (rather than unpatriotic) entities. For purposes of normal operations, except in their local tax liability, they may reside wherever they choose. Corporations have no distinctly patriotic obligations; but they may have distinctive human duties.

But why should profits be the least dispensable of virtues when the popular view is that profits are a form of greed? The answer is plain and compelling: present *profits are offsets to future costs.* Regarded thus, a reasonable amount of them is a necessary duty. Japanese corporations have done well by agreeing with this point of view.

"The Level Playing Field"

The corporation will be dutiful and do good when all other corporations are and do the same. Fair framework conditions, or starting from par with others, has become known as the principle of the Level Playing Field. This principle proclaims that a higher cost of "goodness" is unobjectionable to the corporation if it impinges equally on all competitors. There may in such a case be an immediate need for extra cash to buy new filters and scrubbing-towers; no matter, as long as all others must buy them too. If the field is not level the adoption of all the other virtues is either difficult or unfair to any particular corporation.

But who shall level the playing field if the corporation cannot do so itself without colluding? In some few cases this can be done by legal contract between willing parties. In many more cases by congruent and unaggressive price behavior among competitors – which is to say, by matching rather than by slashing prices. But in many more cases only through laws, statutes and international treaties. In parts of Switzerland all shops must close at certain hours by law, including midday when most working housewives would want conveniently to shop. To hold a sale, or sell at a discount, shops there must apply for an official permit. The same kind of restrictive regulation persists in Germany, whose discount law, the *Rabattgesetz*, forbids price-discounting except in tandem at given periods of the year. (The field has been leveled there for shops-as-producers, to the neglect of people-as-consumers.) On a less trivial scale, GATT, the General Agreement on Tariffs and Trade (now become the WTO or World Trade Organization), the European Union (EU) and the North American Free Trade Area (NAFTA) are attempts to level the field, in addition to other purposes. Still, perhaps naively, I see in the growth of equitable framework conditions, and in the principle of the "level field," evidence for a greater sense of natural justice, and for an economic civilization beyond unbuffered economic Darwinism. The "level field" had not been an equitable principle of business regulation until late in this century.

It is at this point, too, that the corporation is revealed as a sociological entity: it becomes society's concern and, beyond it, the world's concern. It is no longer enough *that* the corporation manufactures useful goods and provides convenient services. *How* is as much the issue. Compare the vast volume of regulations with the relatively small volume of incentives, and it becomes evident that the law is more concerned with division than multiplication.

A conflict, too, appears at the level of the individual: are people to rank more highly as consumers, with their interests, or as employees and producers, with theirs? There is no clear picture yet of a resolution between consumers' and producers' interests. Public sympathy is on the side of both, though both are not always reconcilable. When there is unemployment, sympathy is largely with the unemployed producer; when there is full employment, sympathy is largely on the side of the consumer. But even this distinction is blurred. In the end, the state, and to a lesser but increasing extent the world community, become the flawed and imperfect referees. Though clearly a conflict, it is far from clear how this conflict will be resolved.

Stagnation Capitalism

People start a business because they want to do things, make things, and because they want to make money. I have never met anyone who started a business because he loved administration. Rugged individualism originates well but executes badly.

Let us remember that the corporate principle exists securely but that a secure public philosophy concerning it does not. Earlier in this century, particularly in Europe and before the self-immolation of communism, the idea of private control of private property was not just a debate about its legitimacy. Even more it was a debate about its efficiency.

This was a matter of genuine debate towards the end of the 19th and in the first half of the 20th century. In Britain, few before World War II, and even after, believed that private enterprise was inherently more efficient than national ownership. Postal services, for example, though national, worked well – better than most private service distribution. The same applied to France, Italy and even Scandinavia.

Instability was great between the Wars, inequality greater, poverty and unemployment greatest. Private industry seemed inefficient; anything seemed likely to be more efficient. Expressed urbanely, things were stuck in a sub-optimal equilibrium. Less urbanely, things were rotten. Rights of property were of course an issue; liberty was of course an issue; but whether private corporations were more efficient than public corporations was in doubt.

Not even in the United States and Canada was the higher efficiency of private ownership universally assumed. Franklin Roosevelt's *New Deal* did not assume it. Anti-trust legislation and the break-up of monopolies were chosen to improve efficiency and fairness. The maintenance of private enterprise was preferred because Americans lacked the kind of proletarian mind which turns into a political class. The German sociologist Werner Sombart, in 1906 (in *Why is there no Socialism in the United States?*) unsurprisingly asked why there was no socialism in the United States. He answered his own question partly by saying that every American was at heart an entrepreneur. Most Americans preferred the pursuit of wealth to its equitable distribution.

It was the indomitable belief of most Americans that anyone was free to become rich. In much of Europe at the time this seemed unlikely under either socialism or capitalism. Becoming rich seemed unattainable; but at least things could be made more equal. Equality seemed to be the better liberty. Socialism flourished.

The issue slowly abated. Capitalism began to deliver the goods after World War II. Debate is no longer about the ownership of corporations, but about their nature. By this I do not mean the legal enforcement of honesty, but something more substantial: whether business can be improved by legal instruments. The question deserves an answer now: *how* corporations do things can be adjusted in the public interest; *that* they continue to do something energetic cannot.

When there is no public "propensity to consume" there is little business "inducement to invest." Ideally, policy and laws could help. Unfortunately, government first looks at its nation's affairs and proclaims the virtues of its own generosity; it then looks at the size of its purse and proclaims parsimony to be a greater virtue still.

Costs Are Inside The Corporation; So Is Civilization

Business was, for me as for many, an easy profession to enter. Business proved, for me as for many, a difficult profession to master. It revealed new aspects all the time. No business deal was exactly the same as the one before it. None was an exact precedent for the next deal. There were many facile misconceptions to be overcome: clever tricks did not turn out to be the same as good judgement, high adventure did not turn out to be the same as judicious venture, quick money did not turn out to be the same as long money, wisdom turned out to be the better part of wit, and common duty turned out to be part of the duty to my own business. All this was in addition to a knowledge of techniques, of law, finance, costing, pricing, products and markets, which are to business what anatomy is to medicine. Unlike the human skeleton, every business has a different set of bones.

The solution for corporations is more likely to be found in an internalization of civilization than in external regulation. By this I mean that corporate culture is an enhancement but no substitute for general culture. What gives the Japanese system strength is that the separate cultures of its corporations are intensifications of the common mentality of the Japanese nation. Microsoft and Hewlett-Packard have strong corporate cultures because these enhance and express the best of American civilization. Mercedes-Benz and BMW have strong corporate cultures because these enhance and express the best of German civilization. Anglo-Dutch (Shell) has a strong corporate culture because it blends the best of British and Dutch civilizations. The taproot of the corporate tree appears to need a native soil. I hasten to add that this does not turn the tree into a patriotic plant whose seeds fall only into local ditches.

As an incidental crosscurrent to the above, steelmen from one country speak the language of steel with steelmen from other countries, or oilmen oil, or bankers banking, because there are cultures of industry which are beyond nationality. I found little difficulty, even in communist Albania in the early 1980s, to speak of drill pipe as a common interest and to share the satisfactions of common understanding. The quarry being similar, the pack tends also to be similar.

Mankind as God-kind

In the early 1960s, Robert Merton warned that ours was becoming "a civilization committed to the quest of continually improved means to carelessly examined ends" – technologically, culturally and in business.[1] Others added to the warning. The American educator Robert Hutchins was similarly concerned that our civilization had acquired the habit of believing that "nothing is any more important than anything else." There was, he said, danger in the view that "anything we can do is worth doing."[2]

In the 1990s this concern has become real: for governments, for example, who not long ago wanted to detonate atomic bombs in space to generate power for laser beams that would explode enemy missiles in mid-flight; for corporations, who manipulated the laws of property with "junk" bonds to buy major companies at the cost of crippling them with high and unrepayable debt.

Civilization demands self-restraint. In a sense, civilization *is* self-restraint. And therefore, to internalize civilization into the

values of the corporation is a passable remedy. As in the case of Henry Ford in the 1920s, or Solomon Brothers in New York in the late 1980s, to substitute a corporation's arrogant and special credo for the credos of a civilized society is neither a passable nor lasting remedy. Not all that can be done need be done, even with genetic engineering and its great promise for the human race.

With the discovery of unimpoverishable energy, the uncoding of the human genome, with bio-molecular engineering, and with the reach of corporations to reorder human destiny, *we* must assume responsibility.

More Little Foxes in the Vineyard

There are several unstartling and old-fashioned conclusions.

First and above all, good results come from full mastery of one's trade and from deep interest in it. Beethoven is unlikely to have written the Ninth Symphony in a fit of boredom. I was pleased to hear the CEO of a large chain of bakeries say that he loved baking. The idea that a good manager can immediately switch to manage anything is fiction; unless, of course, it is believed that ratios and balance sheets reveal the secrets of the universe – in which case the world's businesses could all be run by experts in accountancy.

The **second** conclusion is that good work becomes better work when filtered through a civilized mind. By a civilized mind I mean a general interest in affairs, in human needs and private satisfactions. This does not necessarily mean academic education in the arts; nor necessarily graduation from a business school where people often acquire the overweening impression that money is itself a commodity to be packaged seductively and made ready for sale. Some "derivative" financial instruments, derived from other financial instruments, themselves derived from yet other financial instruments, are an example. Somewhere buried at the base of the pyramid, leveraged and almost invisible, are real equity, interest, or commodities.

Money is more than a commodity. It is a summation of work, saving and achievement. It deserves solicitude more than clever packaging. Like happiness, it is the end result of other activities.

The **third** conclusion concerns loyalty. Employees and managers are on the whole more loyal to their corporation than corporations are loyal to them. When times are favorable, corporations can be great and good. When times are bad, corporations prove to be fair-weather friends: facts then drown out sentiments.

Loyalty is bred by a sense of continuous participation. Management involves the management not only of people, but also of the intimate practical knowledge and insights they have acquired. Management by remote control is bound to remain remote. How is it that corporate managements spend millions on quantitative information systems, but make such scant use of the qualitative information in the minds of their customers and suppliers, and even less use of the knowledge of those who work in their factories and offices?

The **fourth** conclusion is that the paradigm of the corporation has been much too masculine. Gender is an irrelevance in business.

My **fifth** conclusion is this: trade and labor unions have been cast, and have cast themselves, in the role of antagonists of management, and *vice versa*, when in reality there is a necessary community of interest between the one and the other. A counter-example is the moderate and sensible *Mitbestimmungsrecht*, the Codetermination Act of the German Federal Republic. It established that each corporation's Supervisory Board shall have the same number of workers' representatives as stockholders' representatives, with an additional member chosen by agreement between the two. This *Aufsichtsrat* also appoints one member of the executive management of the corporation, the *Vorstand*. The arrangement has on the whole worked sensibly and well. Though it has now, perhaps, become too static, it served Germany well for many years.

"Our stability is but balance, and conduct lies in the masterful administration of the unforeseen."[3] My **sixth** conclusion, therefore, concerns the sustenance of freshness. Paradoxically, this implies that systematic change, whatever its other advantages or disadvantages, is a necessary condition of equilibrium. I do not say that every new broom must sweep clean to demonstrate its new authority, but that there is, in almost every corporation, a backlog of the unfulfilled *Important* which was put on dusty shelves in favor of some demonstrably *Urgent* at the time.

The proposition is less paradoxical than may appear. People quit, retire, are replaced; markets change, production methods change, processes change, materials change. Looked at obliquely, competition *is* change. (The statement is not tautological: competition also gives direction to change.) Prolonged routine – much the same way for much the same pay – is deadening. It breeds claims to "proprietary" rights in the *status quo ante*, which, when once established, induces false conservation in employees and management alike. I have also observed that excessively proud mastery of their trade can blind its masters to its vanishing. It may seem unfair that the streamlined and elegant procedures which we have tried so hard to install turn out to be perfect solutions only for the problems of the past. Unfair, perhaps, but that is how it is.

One of the reasons why change is necessary for the equilibrium of corporations is that they have become pluralist entities. Purposes, once simple, are now multiple. Profit has, of course, remained a constant purpose. But even profits are overlaid by the need for profits-for-continuance rather than merely profits-for-the-record.

Profits-for-continuance are the prime aim of Japanese corporations. Japan is a commercial society of managers, by managers, for managers. *Jomukais*, executive committees of managers, are more interested in continued growth, survival, and long-term competitiveness than in immediate profitability. Japan's cultural overlays must not disguise the fact that her culture has been adapted almost wholly to the service of strong commercial and industrial structures. Where it failed, it was through greed, not principle.

The Tides of Competition

Keynes observed, as early as 1926,[4] that it has "been the tendency of big enterprise to socialize itself" and that "the general stability and reputation of the institution" mattered more than maximum profit for stockholders. As we saw in Chapter 1, his was not a solitary voice in the early 20th century.

Progress since then has been mixed. In 1932, two shrewd observers, Adolf Berle and Gardiner Means, pointed out that the management of major corporations had passed from owners to managers, and that ownership had become divorced from control: "The unseen hand of Adam Smith [has been] replaced by the visible hand of business bureaucracy."[5]

Forty-five years later, Alfred Chandler[6] carefully documented the changes which had been noted by Keynes, Berle and Means, and others. Chandler traced the transition from the "invisible hand" of the market to the "visible hand" of corporate control over segments of the market. I shall have to use a very broad brush to summarize the long, detailed and well-documented sweep of his argument.

Chandler's propositions were these: When *administrative* coordination began to yield better results than reliance on the outside market, and when *economic* volume had risen to a sufficient level, enterprises internalized. This is to say that they substituted planned allocations made inside the firm for allocations that had previously been left to the outside market. Put simply, they could now do things, and make things, by themselves and for themselves. Such "internalization" within a single enterprise became possible when a managerial hierarchy had arisen. In due course the hierarchy itself became a source of permanence, power and continued growth. Salaried managers became increasingly technical and professional, and management separated from ownership. Management preferred policies of long-term stability and growth to current profit maximization. Finally, it grew to dominate major sectors of the economy and thus transformed them.

The attentive reader may have raised an eyebrow at the penultimate sentence. Is long-term stability and growth in the mid-1990s still preferred to current profit maximization? Twenty-five or more years ago, American corporations (and some British, Canadian, and Australian corporations) did prefer the long term to the short. Then, alas, they often responded resignedly to competitive threats from abroad. Having been helped by the American government's inexplicable pride in the inflated value of the dollar in the 1980s, and having lost courage for the longer term, American corporations lapsed into immediacy. It was a self-defeating policy. Promptly, the Japanese had the courage to see that Americans had lost theirs. Fortunately, many American corporations have now returned to Chandler's broader findings and have begun to right themselves.

By now, perhaps, the world may have begun to overcome the plague of distortions which descended on it from bad fiscal and financial management by governments: high interest rates in some countries, low interest rates in others, high inflation rates in some countries, low inflation rates in others, so that currencies were not traded on what could be bought with them, but on what they yielded in quick appreciation. Other things being equal, if real interest and inflation rates converged throughout the world, speculative money movements would turn profitless and diminish. Fundamentals would again determine, and true Purchasing Power Parities would again prevail. In the days of Bretton Woods (from the end of World War II until 1972) the brokerage fees of international currency dealers was one sixty-fourth of one percent. No more than that was in it.

An equally attentive reader may not accept that the "invisible hand" of Adam Smith, Berle and Means, and Alfred Chandler, was replaced internationally by the "visible hand" of corporate managements in the 1980s and 1990s. While corporate bureaucracy may have tried to rule within one country, it failed to rule in the world. The gains made in the last thirty years by Japan, Singapore, Taiwan and South Korea were achieved by the giant "invisible hand" of global competition. "Internalization" of control within corporations has been ineffective against the flows of trade, and even less effective against international currency movements.

Until recently, Germany had a particular form of efficient "internalization:" by the "banks as prefects."[7] Representatives of the Big Three – the Deutsche, Commerz, and Dresdner banks – sat on the supervisory boards of most major corporations. They did this partly because they legally voted the shares deposited with them by many small equity owners, and many large. Banks' representatives thus had influence on corporations. In addition, it was impossible for a new corporation to seek outside investors' funds unless it had *at least a year's trading* as a public company behind it. During this period it had to depend wholly on its bank's finance, and at the end of this period its link with this bank tended to continue dependency on it.

Unlike American banks, German banks were also permitted to buy and hold corporate shares. To make this power more reciprocal and comfortable, the banks elected to seat directors of major industrial and commercial corporations on their own boards. It all made for businesslike but fraternal coziness.

German banks combined some of the functions of Japan's MITI (Ministry of International Trade and Industry) with those of the *keiretsu* (the large banking-and-trade-and-industry groupings like Mitsubishi, Mitsui, Sumitomo and C. Itoh).

But in Europe these familial relationships are thinning because financial markets have become global. German corporations are becoming less dependent on Germany's banks. German corporations, as all others, can go where money is cheapest. Germany, like many other countries of continental Europe, has become acquainted with the Anglo-American model of dispersed financial choices. Comfortable, stable, arranged, systemic markets, like Germany's or Switzerland's, which had their roots in historical privilege, are under challenge.

But can the world's economies dispense with "orderly" markets in the long term?

An illustration of the use German banks make of banking and corporate legislation, as well as Other People's Money, is the Klöckner incident of the late 1980s. Klöckner (separate from a steel corporation of the same name), a private trading corporation I knew well, was owned by one family and its trusts and foundations. It was one of Germany's major trading firms, profitable, well administered, with annual sales in many billions. Its principal banker was the Deutsche Bank, Germany's largest.

One of its heads of department took forward positions in crude oil. But instead of rising, the price of oil fell. This manager, without notifying Klöckner's treasury department, doubled his forward contracts in the hope of recouping his anticipated losses. (The contracts were later found in the drawers of his desk.) The matter came to light when first payments became due. By this time contingent losses were estimated at over 600 million deutschmarks – equal to Klöckner's entire capital. The owners, the Henle family, honorably and immediately notified the Deutsche Bank that Klöckner's entire capital had been wiped out and that Klöckner's net worth was zero or less than zero. Since the other departments had meanwhile continued to do normal and profitable business, the bank came to the rescue. It bought Klöckner for one mark and assumed its present and contingent liabilities. The Henle family had lost its invested fortune in Klöckner at a stroke. But the company continued to trade, and the guiltless did not lose their jobs. Some one or two years later, the Deutsche Bank sold the still profitable Klöckner AG to a conglomerate at a gain of more than half a billion marks. There are indeed few substitutes for a very deep pocket.

States Try To Steer, But Knowledge Has Its Foot On The Accelerator

It has also become evident that scientific knowledge is too unconfinable to be "internalized" by any single corporation, however large. As a result, a new "internalization" has appeared: joint research, development, and process cooperation between companies of several nationalities, primarily in computer, aircraft, and other high technologies. Scientific knowledge has proved to be unconfinable: it spills from the inventive minds of one country to those of other countries at the speed of light. Given adequate entrepreneurship and infrastructure, the Comparative Advantage of Nations is yielding to other kinds of borderless comparative advantages.

There is a contradictory exception to this tendency. As the technological intricacy of invention and development increases, patents and copyrights (rather than old industrial skills and experience) are becoming the most valuable properties of corporations. But by their nature and purpose, patents and copyrights are an officially sanctioned exclusion of competitors. Patents and copyrights are today what charters for monopoly corporations were a few centuries ago.

Some unintended consequences may arise from this. In

growing measure, intellectual property is becoming a corporation's most valuable treasure. Since intellectual property can be officially protected from imitation, its protection may become a hurdle to free trade – at a time when other barriers are being lowered. I do not argue that intellectual property does not deserve protection; but that patents, by unleveling the playing field, may become increasingly powerful weapons in restraint of national and international competition. Similar to this is a modern tendency to other kinds of contractual monopolization. Exclusive rights to non-intellectual properties, such as sole television rights for sports events, are equal denials of accessibility.

States, in the course of the centuries and in the name of kings, secured an Erastian supremacy over churches. Now, in the name of the people, states assert themselves over the temples of business. The device of governmental industrial policy grows by regulation and legal fiat. It is a stronger device than the "indicative planning" once fashionable in France. Government does not now participate in the cost of development. It only compels where monies shall be spent (or not spent) by private industry. In the United States, for example, federal and state governments impose regulations for low-energy-using refrigerators and other consumer durables. Prescriptions are in force for automobiles with reduced fuel consumption and emissions. The Air Resources Board of the State of California initially demanded that by the year 2003 ten percent of all automobiles shall be ZEVs, "zero emission vehicles." In practice this would mean that ten percent of all motor vehicles will be powered by electricity. They will be: the state of California has not only forced development, but also forcibly provided a market for the developed product (unless its legislature weakens). The future shape of high-definition television is subject to legal decrees. The European Union issues numerous regulations that govern standards. This rules out non-conforming alternatives and confines the field of competition to those adapting or ruled in. All this may not be called "industrial policy." But though it may not be called one, it is one. The playing field remains level but the goalposts have been moved. They will undoubtedly be moved again.

Summary

Present corporate purposes will become less tenable in a more crowded, more intensive, well-moneyed but rat-pack world – a world of economic transformations and denser encroachments; a world in which the profit-seeking procedures of corporations affect not only wealth, but, increasingly, ways of life.

In 1942, Schumpeter predicted the "creative self-destruction" of capitalism, its bureaucratization, followed by socialism. This neither happened, nor is it likely to occur. But the frequent persistence of corporate incivility, predatoriness and self-gratification may no longer be accepted. The purposes of profit may have to be reviewed. Profits will have to serve not for luxuriant surpluses, but as offsets to future costs and for continuance, growth and survival. Depreciation Allowances are in place (in taxation practice) to provide for the renewal of wearing or worn-out plant and equipment; similarly, in the future, profits should be regarded as a corporate Appreciation Allowance. The concept of Return on Capital Employed may have to stand alongside the additional criterion of a Social Return on Capital Employed.

The discordance, too, between the short-termist financial view of money as a tradeable commodity – "money makes money" – and the broader industrial view of "money plus capital plant *plus work* makes money" must find a juster reconciliation; lest the myopia of the first ends in partial blindness for the business system as a whole.

As in an earlier counter-reformation, faith in quick gain (to buy indulgences for CEOs) may have to yield to good faith, good works, and ampler purposes.

8

The Civility of Corporations

In most of the West, the marvels of technology are only wanted if they sustain and promote acceptable values. People continue to cherish old ideals of peace, liberty, fraternity, order, and the pursuit of happiness. Progress is welcome, but not if it imperils a hard-won status quo.

But conservation is not the same as conservatism, nor is stability the same as invariance. Even the conservative anti-revolutionary Edmund Burke reminded the late 18th century that "a state without the means of some change is without the means of its conservation." If this is allowed, and if the direction of change is acceptable, there remains only the distinction between desirable change and desirable rate of change.

Democratic capitalism permits things to be done, but depends on things actually being done – largely by business as a main agent of change. Business, however, itself depends on many independent visions;

it depends on optimism to transform potentiality into actuality; it depends on willingness to venture; it depends on an absence of social inertia; it depends on personal maturity; it depends on willingness to take responsibility; it depends on reciprocal trust; it depends on keeping promises and contracts; it depends on an absence of corruption; it depends on its own civility; it depends on a fair dominion of laws. Where what can and should be done is not sufficient cause for doing it, business runs the risk of turning into a barren order of society.

The Civility of Corporations

Decapitation as a Cure For Headaches: Cutting Labor Costs

Ever since Henry Ford, in 1914, decided to pay his workers five dollars a day – two-and-a-half times the average rate which was then paid in the United States – and yet built cars more cheaply than any other manufacturer, corporations have had good reasons to abandon the belief that low wages alone yield an important comparative advantage either domestically or internationally. The belief may still be true in some cases but is destined to diminish. Far more than the cost of labor is involved, and even a vanishingly low labor cost will fail to make Ethiopia, Mongolia and Albania into fit competitors of Hewlett-Packard, Siemens and Boeing, nor will it ensure the future of Mexican *maquiladoras*, cheap workshops for Americans and Japanese, beyond a decade or so. On the other hand, Germany, which has very high pay-roll costs per labor hour, has been a major exporter of tailored clothes – the making of which is traditionally thought to be labor-intensive. Singapore prospered by deliberately raising wages in the late 1970s while raising skills. The labor content of computer software, aircraft, biotechnology, and so on – things made laboriously in expensive countries – is immense. But these well-paid sectors have made countries not less but more competitive. The comparative advantage of nations and of corporations is not made by hoes and hammers, nor is sweat a substitute for invention and investment.

There was a time – in Europe in the 17th and 18th centuries – when the low-wage competition of one country could indeed fatally afflict another. The industry and commerce of Venice, for example, declined in the 17th century because of Dutch and English competition in the general appeal and price of goods. Restrictive guilds of artisans had held back renewal of designs and had kept wages high, while private monopoly and rigid public fiscal policies had kept prices high. About one hundred years later the Netherlands suffered a similar fate: public revenues from excise had forcibly grown higher than England's, though England had twice the population. The textile industries of Leyden and Haarlem, and the potteries of Delft, thriving a hundred years before, virtually vanished by the middle of the 18th century, having yielded to England's lower costs. There was no quick escape to the efficiencies of refined technologies – of which there were few. The few that were were slow to grow.

This of course is not the whole story. Much survived, and Dutch money was lent massively to other countries. Much Dutch wealth went to the making of England of the 18th and early 19th century, and elsewhere. The circle then turned in on itself: after the middle of the 19th century England became a banker to the world far more than banker to Britain.

What emerges is that in a non-industrial or in a low-industrial world, foreign wage competition is usually fatal; whereas in today's high-industrial world, wage differentials between countries are neither fatal nor decisive. According to GATT, the General Agreement on Tariffs and Trade, the loss of jobs by advanced economies to the Third World has so far been only five percent on average. They were, in general, jobs of low quality. (Things are made more complex because some national economies, instead of exporting jobs, import guest laborers to do disagreeable work.) Far more jobs were, and still are, lost through domestic automation.

Remarkably, the real investment of industrial countries in other industrial countries accounts for more than three-quarters of all their foreign investments. Advanced economies – those of the USA, of Europe and Japan – send from two- to three-fifths of their exports to less developed countries, and gain jobs. The less developed countries spend their gain on products and machines from the advanced economies. Trade increases, and so do industries. And the best customers of advanced "high-cost" economies are other advanced "high-cost" economies.

None of this will of course be true if Western corporations prefer cheap labor to investment; if they choose to be content with old technology because they lack the will to renew themselves, or because they have no money to do so. Corporations will choose their own paths. But it is certain that those who procrastinate will be the first to crumble.

Corporations Tending to Become Sets of ad hoc Associations

Corporate conduct is changing. Chandler's "internalization" is in partial retreat. Corporations are digging into the external human resources of society. Consultants and lobbyists as commissioned intermediaries fill the interstices between the planned corporation, society and government. Lobbies are popularly regarded as specious public relations agencies hired by a corporation to sway politics in favor of the corporation's preferences – and often are. But it would be a mistake to imagine that all consultants and lobbyists can be hired as drudges and touts to do as they are told and never answer back. An intelligent consultant or lobbyist soon becomes an advisor to his client corporation on good or bad business strategies. He becomes more than an intercessor for his corporate clients.

In addition, some who work in corporations are only intellectual participants. Among them are people held together by networks of common interest. The Labor Secretary in Clinton's Administration, Robert Reich, calls them "symbolic analysts." They are interchangeable between corporations: computer programmers and system analysts, internal auditors, internal consultants, artists, accountants and lawyers. They perform their specialist intellectual tasks and migrate to the next corporation which needs their services. They admit, as Peter Drucker pointed out,[1] their functional responsibility to do a job for the corporation, but they are no longer its employees in any traditional sense. Their loyalty is more to their professional assignment than to the corporation that hired them.

There is a parallel to this in the work of science and arts correspondents, columnists, stringers and syndicated writers in the world of newspaper journalism. An early parallel were the floating population of educated wandering scholars of the medieval church, which was thus both a universal *and* a virtual corporation.

As in newspapers, the knowledge worker in a corporation is "a colleague and an associate rather than a subordinate." His importance is immense because the genius who installs the procedural software for a bank, airline or travel agency determines for years how the company will operate.

There is a present and future consequence of this. Given that their loyalty is more to a professional assignment than to the corporation that hired them, and given that what they do is to transmute ideas into saleable product, what more profitable use can they make of these assignments? If they developed computer software for one master, it is certain that there is inside them always more of it where that came from. They can start in business on their own and often do so. Knowledge breeds derived knowledge; and derived knowledge breeds derived corporations.

There is another loosening of the ties of loyalty and good faith between employer and employees within the corporations. It stems from four events. One, mentioned elsewhere, is that most new investment displaces people. The second is that the concept of life-long service and job security cannot withstand the assaults of recession, even in Japan. The third is that temporary bargains of adherence are displacing bargains of permanent belonging. Corporations hire other corporations, domestic or foreign, to do a job by contract which was previously internal. Or specialists incorporate themselves, and trade not as individuals but as corporations. No pension obligations and fiduciary duties are incurred by those who use them and no loyalty, but only contractual performance, is owed by those who are thus hired.

Lastly, the better a corporation adapts to change, the less certain of a secure job (at every level) those become who work in it. Surprisingly, corporations tend to see forthcoming change more clearly than balance. The edges of change are vaguely visible; areas of stability only become evident in retrospect. And so corporations are more ready to assume that the times are in flux, and are more ready to offer limited contracts, contingent or part-time work rather than steady jobs. That is almost all right in times of full employment, but not all right at other times. The present consequence is a general absence, in individuals and in society, of what has become known as the feel-good factor. The long-term social implications of this now common sentiment are as yet unclear, but may be onerous if it turns out that high unemployment rates are structural.

Notably, most high-tech corporations – those that employ people of high academic quality – are reluctant to downsize. Confidence suffers, work suffers, and the penalty of insecurity is far too great. Even William Roche, the advocate of downsizing, now believes that sackings destroy too much. This once-fashionable tide is ebbing. The best way to be slim is to stay slim in the first place.

Sub-corporations Within Other Corporations

The future may bring extensions of the corporate idea. More than forty years ago, when young, naive and new to business, it occurred to me that there might be advantages in hiring people not as individuals but as private corporations – availed of all the means the law provides for carrying losses forward, paying dividends, expanding by the recruitment and training of additional working partners, and so forth. Large corporations might then (in part) become assemblies of sub-units composed of incorporated private enterprises, chosen by competitive bids to serve the large corporation. They would perform defined processes competitively within it, and pay it rent for the use of space, machines and equipment. Many years later I saw some examples of this idea in action: at a steel pipe mill in Japan, a separate corporation cut the threads on pipes made by the mill, and equipped them with couplings. It was housed at the end of the principal pipe mill's production line, was integral to the production process, but was run by an independently owned company. Perhaps my naive idea was less naive than my then lack of confidence had me believe.

But despite the risks, and given that a venture capital market continues to be available, the birthrate of new corporations will increase. It is sometimes true that large corporations with a spread of many products have a greater tolerance of risk than small corporations with few. As now, when risk becomes too great for them to bear, small corporations will be bought by, merged or amalgamated into large. But large corporations will not ingest all small corporations. The small corporation has always found new nurseries for its ingenious children. As modern markets and products become more intricate and complex, so more market segments, interstices and niches appear. The small corporation also has another advantage, which is that by their nature, all corporations prod people into coordinated work; but large corporations, more than small, must spend more of their time making them work together.

And yet there are doubts. No platoons of consultants, no troops of real or "symbolic" analysts, no battalions of sub-contractors and suppliers, can be a substitute for the immediate knowledge of a corporation's own managers – managers who constantly breathe the air of change. There is no complete substitute for this, and no complete alternative to a sufficient degree of management watchfulness, management competence, management's humanism, and management density. As to management density, Japan spends a higher proportion of cost on sales than its competitors. The huge apparatus of Japan's large trading corporations manages most of its exports and imports at great expense and with constant presence. No country has a higher density of international marketers and export administrators than Japan; yet the return has so far justified its cost.

Ledgers as Managers: Accountancy is not Leadership

Bureaucracy's anatomies are stiff. Bureaucracy clings; it blocks new structures and new purposes. It can measure all results except its own. When Management by Accountancy is allowed to dominate, corporations turn into short-term profit seekers. Alfred D. Chandler, in *The Visible Hand,* outlined three historical transformations: an early dominance by the entrepreneur; then a short stage of financial dominance of industry by such as John Pierpont Morgan; then the emergence of managerial and administrative dominance. Even now, the tendency at any given time in any given corporation is for one of these to dominate over the other two.

I concede that some aggressive management rams can be as bad as flocks of bureaucratic sheep. When a business leader displays excessive financial dexterity in mergers and acquisitions; when he lets asset valuation become his only gauge of

value; when, as is usual in such exercises, he puts the corporation heavily in debt; when, as is also usual in such exercises,
people become an irrelevant "value" to him, then all that his
dexterity in the end achieves is a weakened and distrusted
company, his own ill reputation, and, worst of all for him, the
low esteem of capital markets.

Not only communist economies were stifled by bureaucracy. It also happened in nationalized industries in Western
countries. Many nationalized industries in Europe were not
allowed to diversify from, say, coal mining or ship building to
other purposes. Their structures froze. Large private industries
have shown the same tendency. In the second half of the 19th
century, John Pierpont Morgan had "consolidated" the railroads
into a mighty empire. Even at the beginning of 1930, the assets
(gross less depreciation) of rail transport corporations constituted 46 percent, or nearly half, of all "billion-dollar" non-
banking corporations in the United States. They failed to adapt
and diversify, and are no longer on the list of the mighty. Corporations which defined themselves as defense contractors
rather than as engineering industries declined when armaments
were reduced. Had the United States Steel Corporation (now
USX) not bought its way into the energy industry by acquiring
Marathon Oil some years ago, it might not have stanched a yet
more serious decline. In the end, structure-dominated entities
tend to lose to purpose-driven entities. Structure-domination
happened to the Soviet Union: founded on intransigent ideas, it
mummified into intransigent bureaucracy, and crumbled. Contrary to Engels's Marxian hopes, while the state did not wither,
ideas did.

But nor does this support either Joseph Schumpeter's[2] or
Robert Heilbronner's[3] prophecies on the future of the business
system and the corporation. Schumpeter, in 1942, wrote that
"creative [self-]destruction," bureaucratization, then socialism,
would be the fate of capitalism; Heilbronner, in 1976, that a slow

decline like the Roman Empire's, superseded by a new "religious orientation," would be its fate.

There is no evidence of either outcome. Nationalization has turned into an unpromising alternative. Under it, the concept of the state and of the corporation was merged: the state was in danger of becoming a quasi-corporation. It suffered from the weaknesses of all monopolies – from the East India Company to the Soviet empire.

Corporations Are Themselves Becoming Mixed Economies

"Socialization" continues, but is "social"-ization now. The connotation of the word is no longer the same. It no longer means a change of "ownership of the means of production, distribution and exchange" from private hands to the state. It means instead a humanizing of standards of behavior, a mixed economy, a social market economy. Examples abound: environmental standards, protection of wildlife and endangered species, the regulation of finance and banking, the "strict" interpretation of product liability, the long approval route for pharmaceuticals and "new" food, barriers to "new" plants and "new" animals devised by genetic science, and the sustenance of the life of the sick.

It can be argued that this humanization is beyond the limits of commercial endurance, and that it leads to stultification. But these limits will continue to be tested by society. Like states, corporations have become mixed economies.

Clearly, the question of the Level Playing Field again arises if some countries are stricter in their regulation of corporations than others. I do not contest the need for uniform rules of conduct to preserve the world's environment; but neither do non-uniform rules of conduct help industrial initiative. Many now argue that the courts in the United States – more than those of other countries – damage the nation's business by over-generous jury awards in personal injury suits and torts – to compensate, but also to wash away sin. It has been estimated that in the United States the potential liability insurance included in the price of a ladder is higher than the cost of the metal of which it is made, and that a manufacturer's potential liability insurance for a small airplane equals half its cost. Behind the pleas for equity for mankind is a plea for equity for corporations.

Knowledge Transforms its Source

Corporations are not enduring monoliths; they come and they go, make their appearances and say their farewells. Their purposes change; the composition of their managements and their employees alters more quickly than the natural flux of generations. Their power is opposed by countervailing powers. Singly, some of them abuse their power; most of them, surprisingly, do not. But though business in aggregate is a powerful transmuting force in society, corporations are themselves self-transforming, pliant, altered by time and circumstance. They are continuously remolded by technology, by the demands of the market, and by competition. They are, above all, remolded because they are centers of knowledge – knowledge which continues to advance, deepen, evolve, transform and transmute. This implies that corporations will more cause than follow social changes – unlike traditions, national moods, churches, parliaments and other institutions. The difference between the knowledge worker and other workers is that he shapes the work that shapes the work of other workers.

But though corporations may command competition for a while, they must obey it in the end. Corporations are useful, not moral, entities by origin; but they are molded, willy-nilly, to social utility by social evolutions.

Their primary objective, profit, while highly useful, is neither noble nor ignoble. The limits of the power of money being what they are, money should teach humility to those capable of understanding these limits, while those incapable of understanding them will not understand anything else about business either. It is hard to disagree with Dr. Johnson's view that making money is one of the more innocent occupations of mankind and that the world has known many worse employments. Commercial corporations are blamed for their materialism; but we cannot talk of art and play the grand piano all the time. Corporations generate incomes for many, and the sense of dignity that comes with sufficient private means is more than just materialism.

"Service Without Kindness" and the Future

But the concept of the corporation is shot through with ambiguities. In 1960, the public corporation was said to be "no more individual than an infantry division."[4] Much earlier, David Hume had said that it did "service to another without bearing him a real kindness."

The largest corporation shareholders are not individuals, but institutions like pension funds or insurance corporations who serve the interests of their own shareholders and stakeholders. They behave as though their interest lay less in the long-term fate of the corporations in which they have a holding, but more in the capital appreciation of their own portfolios; hence they buy and sell their stocks and shares for transient gain. And thus "owners" have become speculators; gamekeepers turned poachers.

But increasingly, with alteration in the spirit of the age, it is becoming clear that the corporation is society's creature, and that it has been molded as much by social and political as by business purposes. The tendency of the law to let the corporation mold itself is a tribute to its bias towards freedom. But though the law has left the corporation in this condition, it must not rest in the belief that freedom will always shape it to perpetual good purpose. Corporations still need referees with whistles.

Although owners have lost their position of personal responsibility for the proper conduct of the corporation, and although managers are now the only identifiable body capable of doing so, little legal onus attaches to managers who manage legally but badly. The law only demands that they be a) attentive, b) faithful, and c) prudent – which is what it requires of any humble servant. Except in cases of wrongful trading, outright fraud, or *ultra vires* actions (deeds surpassing the legal limits of their powers) no action is or can be generally taken against them and the corporation's board for beta-minus, indifferent performance. Prodigious attention to their own self-interest, remuneration and bonuses is in itself unpunishable by the law. Therefore good faith and competence is simply assumed to be something which, God willing, the market will supply.

But the market may fail in this duty. It cannot well be expected, Adam Smith remarked, that the managers of other people's money should watch over it with the same "anxious vigilance" as if it were their own.[5] In the early part of this century Walter Rathenau expressed the hope, cited elsewhere, that "as a motive force the covetousness [of management] has been completely superseded by the sense of responsibility." Yet Adam Smith's much lower expectations continue to evoke at least the same degree of anxious vigilance today as they did then.

"Other People's Money," OPM, includes not only equity shareholders and holders of preference shares, but also subordinated lenders of the funds the corporation borrows (such as "senior" creditors who are secured by the corporation's assets, and "junior," unsecured creditors), bondholders, pensioners and future pensioners, employees with wages and salaries due to them, and, not least, trade creditors and all such persons with major legal title. As tax collectors and watchdog regulators (when they are not bemused by spurious ideologies) governments too are vigilant for the population.

Corporations may also have egregious contingent liabilities – future ghosts haunting the present. These liabilities are monies which may be due to individuals or groups for false or faulty representations, for environmental damage, damage to individual health, or potential hazard posed by inadequate products – asbestos, oil spills, release of noxious gases or liquids in industrial accidents, product liabilities, radiation – sufficiently large, if courts so decide, to put both guilty and innocent companies into bankruptcy.

All these stakeholders have a security claim on bits and pieces of the corporation. There are no doubts and no ambivalence when the firm is a going concern: shareholders receive their dividends, bondholders their interest and redemptions at maturity, pensioners their pensions; contingent liabilities are settled when they become actual. The question "Who owns the company?" is neither raised in profitable times, nor is an answer wanted. All is well when claimants' explanations of fair dealing are satisfactorily met.

"The shareholder in the modern corporate situation has surrendered a set of definite rights for a set of indefinite expectations."[6] It can almost be said that the corporation as a "going concern" leases the stockholder's equity capital at an undetermined rent and for an indeterminate period, and that he is quite content with this. Since the stock's owner can regain liquidity by selling his "bundle of expectations" on stock exchanges for ready money, why should he also concern himself with the control of the corporation? He is satisfied to let management have its rights of possession-without-ownership and to let it play Cat's Cradle with the corporation as long as it plays the game for satisfactory dividends and share appreciation.

But the thick sludge of "ownership" rises to the top when things go wrong. The corporation's stockowners, its creditors and its employees vie for preference when a company is faced with bankruptcy – or *Konkurs, fallimento,* voluntary liquidation, involuntary liquidation, insolvency, receivership, trusteeship, Chapter 11, Chapter 7, "composition," "rearrangement," "restructuring," *redressement judiciaire,* "administration," "reorganization," and other periphrases for a hard reality.

Broadly, as to preference in bankruptcy proceedings: in the United States, "Chapter 11" puts creditors on anxious hold, whereas in Britain and in Germany the law inclines towards them. It inclines towards management in France; towards employees and shareholders in Japan. And though most countries prefer composition and private settlement to public enforcement, the sludge of mine-and-thine is thick in either case. As may be expected, debts to government are everywhere at the head of the queue.

When the corporation is a going concern, the laws of property are almost silent. But when the murmuring begins, the property rights of claimants assert themselves from all directions and all the tongues of law begin to speak.

In summary, the stockholders of the corporation "own" the corporation's balance sheet – all that is in "the womb of equity." They do not "own" the corporation's profit-and-loss account, whence profit came or loss occurred, and who decided either.

As to its employees and "workers," it was once held that much should be owed to them because their labour creates "value." It is difficult to sustain this notion in a world of intricate technology in which neither employees nor workers (a now peculiar word) understand the whole that they are making. Apart from payment in return for the value they add, what is owed to them is consideration by reason of their membership of a social entity rather than by reason of their mechanical manipulation of a product in the making.

When it Endures: The Enduring Corporation

In the last sentence of *The Modern Corporation and Private Property*, published at the time of the New Deal in 1932, Berle and Means concluded that business practice was increasingly assuming the aspect of "economic statesmanship." They also suggested that "the law of corporations [] might well be considered as a potential constitutional law for the new economic state."

The modern temper is warier of "economic statesmanship" than they were. No one has lately issued a request for the law of corporations to become the constitutional law of a nation. No voices of business have dared to demand as much as did Berle and Means. I.S. Shapiro, a Ford Foundation trustee and Chairman of DuPont from 1974 to 1981, for example, said that society now writes the ground rules for business and that corporations have become "more ruled than ruling." He only asked that the private sector could and should contribute more than it has to the public policy process.[7]

From time to time, the need for legal reform is compelling. Business churns the soil of society; and therefore, as I have said elsewhere, as long as government accepts the churnings and transformations made by the workings of the business system, it must also accept that these will change the nature of government. But beyond this, four reasons compel me to give only sparing acceptance for an imposed reform of corporations for political or "ideological" reasons.

The **first** is that "fresh thinking" and stale thoughts often go together. This is an age in which entrenched institutions are told to yield to new liberties. Yet when it comes to practice such ideas often turn out to be mere surplus products of other establishments.

The **second** reason is that corporations are the complex creations of a complex civilization in which complexities increase rather than diminish. This was exemplified by the US

Federal Administration's attempt to simplify the American tax code during the Reagan presidency in the 1980s. Instead of slimming, the tax code fattened. (In fairness to the Reagan administration, this was partly due to embellishments by Congress.) Reform is likely to be more effective and less unsettling if it is practically organic rather than philosophically synthetic. For example, a noticeable convergence between Common and "Roman" law concepts concerning commerce is happening in Europe. Judges, "when presented with situations which seem to demand a remedy, will, if untrammelled by statute, usually attempt to find a solution."[8]

The **third** reason is also the result of increasing complexity and wealth. Corporations have not become more like ordinary persons, but a great many ordinary persons have become more like corporations. Millions of individual citizens of industrialized countries have assets worth many thousands of dollars, marks, francs, lire or pounds, or an assortment of all these. Their properties are multiple and intricate; like corporations, they own a lot and they owe a lot: mortgages, equity in real property, shares, tax-exempt and non-exempt bonds, cars, furnishings and art, pension expectations and entitlements, insurances, capital appreciations, dividends, incoming interest, outgoing interest, tax liabilities and tax refunds, tax-sheltered investments, bank loans, overdrafts, expectations under one or more wills, and so on. They have all the marks of the corporation except product, and all the needs that corporations have for accountancy, legal advice and the planning of succession and estates. A radical reform of corporation law would involve a radical reform of many laws concerning individuals.

The **fourth** reason is that planning by corporations, however imperfect, has yet in recent decades been generally better than planning by governments. Little that corporations have done has been as culpable as the monetary and fiscal stop-and-go, inflationary management by British governments since

World War II; nothing is as culpable as the mismanagement of the national debt and budgetary deficits by American governments since the 1980s – management which has more than doubled the national debt of the United States in a single decade. Excepting only Japan and Western Europe, the national debt of the United States alone now approximately equals the total gross domestic product of all remaining countries of the world. France, Italy, Greece, Turkey, Spain, most of Latin America and much of Asia, have had, or still have, long periods of incompetence.

In Italy since the 1960s, for example, government became corrupt. Italian business, vigorous as is the nature of its people, tried to overcome this handicap – by ignoring it, or by paying bureaucrats and politicians to let it be. In the end, when sniffle had turned to pneumonia, the nation jibbed and sent the rascals packing. But had it not turned against the sway of thieves and kleptocrats, Italy's further progress would probably have been quenched. And therefore, if the political and economic management of a nation's affairs is consistently rotten, honest corporations cannot succeed; and if they fail the capitalist process cannot proceed. And if this process cannot proceed then groping for tempestuous new economic and political solutions and ideologies will again begin. Capitalism depends on management by government, and even more on management of government.

This statement, I know, is arguable. A historian may point to the commercial-patrician oligarchies of 12th- to 17th-century Europe – to Venice, Florence, Luebeck – and say that they were successful forms of capitalism. Some, he may maintain, like Florence, even were successful industrial capitalisms. But they were not only warlike but also warring, secured by an unforgiving police against their own workers and lower artisans. Some, like Venice, were slavers. They were city states often ruled by established Mafias and Camorras who were not beyond murder and conspiracy. By modern standards they were intolerable. Again, a historian may point to Pinochet's Chile after the destruction of Allende, and he may quote statistics to demonstrate the growth of output and trade under his military dictatorship. But those who know the business Chile did when he was president in the 1970s and 1980s will also know what toadying was required to run one. In Asia, too: in Indonesia it has been self-destructive folly to go against the business inclinations of the highest leadership of government.

Only in the sense that they are under the law are corporations creatures of the law. Laws and charters explain the origin of corporations; they do not explain their evolution. The law never told corporations how to develop their techniques and working practices. These were their own inventions, approved but unpredicted by the law. From the end of the 19th century to the middle of the 20th, the massed impersonal resources of the corporation, rather than a grouping of owners, became its predominant feature. But now the corporation's "person"hood is beginning to acquire one characteristic of real persons which was previously missing. Responsibility, imposed or spontaneous, is demanded.

Any enduring social institution must have two qualities: it must be manageable and it must satisfy. Whom the corporation must satisfy is not a question of philosophy: there is more than enough philosophy. It is a question of robust humanity.

Summary and Conclusion

While churches, and even states, the law and the arts, proclaim sacred or ultimate values, corporations have no fundamental, expressly social values of their own (except for constancy in the pursuit of profit as a rough gauge of corporate health).

I have suggested that an answer is to be found in "internalized" civilization. By this, I repeat, I do not mean any abandonment of profit motive, nor high learning and intellectual abstraction for its own sake. I mean a universality, a corporate

universitas of people who search, learn, thrust, and work together, and who remain, in Hume's words, "industrious and
civilized." I also mean that the need for numerous levels of
supervisory management diminishes when all ranks in a corporation are of a mind to understand, search, learn, thrust and
cooperate because they are "industrious and civilized" by
inclination.

A question remains. The corporation has, doubtless,
become a better citizen and neighbor. In many cases it has turned
social conscience into corporate policy. But it has the freedom to
dip into the general pool of resources. This includes the freedom
to dip at will into the pool of people. It accepts some for work
and rejects others. The rejected "comprise the unemployed, the
ill-educated, and the entire residue of human beings who are not
needed by the corporate machine."[9] Some, including this author,
will say that the freedom of the corporation to accept and reject is
not a freedom; it, too, is held in the shackles of the market and
cannot hire as it pleases.

But while this is true of any one corporation, it cannot be
wholly true of a corporate system, because that which radiates
power must radiate conscience. Corporations have the limited
but ultimate right to hire and fire. But governments must pay the
unemployed from taxes collected from the purses of the people.
Therefore, where the deeds of the one are paid for by the purses
of the other, it is not possible to suppose that the freedom of
corporations can be unbounded.

This, if anything, is the deep contradiction in contemporary
capitalism. As long as heaps of humanity are involuntarily
consigned to dumps, society will continue to question both
governments and the corporate constituency, and ask who is
responsible.

The concept of the corporation at work inevitably leads on to the
idea of competition – the subject of the next chapter – and to the

unexpected conclusion that competition is operable partly because of habits of tolerance and partly because of the rules of engagement set by society over many centuries.

9

Tolerance as a Principle
of Competition

" Thou shalt not covet; but tradition approves all forms
of competition. "

A.H. Clough

The eminent 20th-century author, Joseph Schumpeter, described com-
petition within capitalist society as a process of "creative destruction" –
a term which equally suits Darwin's reading of natural evolution.

Competition destroys, then uses the residue to recreate. There the
similarity ends: unlike human society, nature knows nothing of indi-
vidual or corporate rights and duties, nothing of promises and contracts,
nothing of responsibility and reciprocal obligation. But if competition is

destructive, how is the high value assigned to it in one mode of society, capitalism, to be explained?

Competition forces political, economic and democratic debate on the advantages and disadvantages of change and rearrangement. This in turn means negotiation, compromise and bargaining. These in turn mean that power is significantly bounded. Containment makes for a habit of tolerance.

None of these processes are "natural," since nature is not tolerant and does not bargain. But, suitably superintended, competition in human society and especially in business becomes a tool of personal and corporate civility.

Tolerance as a Principle
of Competition

Natural and Social Competition

Not nature but society was first found to be "red in tooth and claw." The idea of Darwinism in society preceded Darwin. Surprisingly, the study of competition in civilization came before the study of competition in nature. The sequence was as follows:

In 1776, Adam Smith first published *An Inquiry into the Nature and Causes of the Wealth of Nations*. It demonstrated the advantages of free trade and commercial competition. The final 5th edition came out in 1789.

In 1798, the Reverend Thomas Robert Malthus, another economist, published the short first edition of his *Essay on the Principle of Population* (anonymously, for some reason). It dealt with the fateful competition between rising populations for inadequate supplies of food. The final 6th edition, considerably longer, came out in 1826.

In 1859, Charles Darwin published *The Origin of Species by Means of Natural Selection*. He had written a sketch of this work on natural competition in 1844, fifteen years before. It is ironical that he hurried to publication in 1859 because of competition: from a need to publish before Alfred Russel Wallace who had come to similar conclusions independently. Wallace, too, had read Malthus; as a result of this reading, he said, "there suddenly flashed upon me the idea of the survival of the fittest."

Malthus had read Adam Smith, and Darwin had read both Smith and Malthus. (Darwin records the precise day: September 28th, 1838. But why only then when Malthus's important book had been available for twelve or more years?) Half a century or so had elapsed between the last edition of Smith's "Wealth" and Darwin's early (1844) unpublished essay on the origin of species.

Smith and Malthus had set competition at the core of much of human life; Darwin set competition at the core of all life. Darwin's reflections on competition in organic life had a great deal to do with Smith's and Malthus's preceding thoughts on human competition. One might even suppose that had the earlier two authors not published their views when they did, Darwin and Wallace might not have come to theirs until later or at all. Many continue to believe that human rivalry is a sort of Darwinism derived from his theory of natural competition. In fact it is clear that theories of human competition preceded theories of natural competition. They may even have suggested them.

It is remarkable that in the 18th and 19th century, a time we now regard as an age of optimism and belief in progress, many of its oracles – Malthus, Ricardo, by implication even Darwin – concluded that life is as brushwood in the fires of nature.

It is also notable that Keynes, the greatest economist of the dismal second quarter of the 20th century, should by comparison have been an optimist who thought that human nature could be managed provided one did not attempt to transmute it.[1]

To offset this optimism, the third quarter of this century produced the *Theory of Games and Economic Behaviour*, which claims that competition makes vain the search for a uniquely best solution for human affairs. The Theory of Games was one of the subjects of Chapter 2.

The Nature of Society is not the Nature of Nature

It is tempting but wrong to say that the laws that govern nature also govern human affairs. It is wrong to suppose, as Malthus almost did, that economic laws ineluctably rule mankind. If this were so, it would reduce to insignificance most religions, every philosopher who ever lived, and all those who proclaimed a hope of progress. It is man's nature to oppose nature and, in T.H. Huxley's words, to check "the cosmic process at every step" – at times successfully.

There is a major difference between the laws of nature and laws concerning society. Laws of nature are discoverable but not alterable. Newton or no Newton, gravity remains gravity. Not so when it comes to economic "laws" – to Malthus who said that while population increases by geometric progression, (1, 2, 4, 8, 16...) food production can only increase arithmetically (1, 2, 3, 4, 5...) – or to Karl Marx.

Marx said that under the laws of capitalism an "immiseration of the masses" is inevitable. Both were wrong. As soon as they were revealed, such economic "laws" were opposed by employees, amended by legislatures, suspended by science, and rendered harmless or less stinging. Natural laws continue whether known or unknown; but economic laws cease to operate when revealed and effectively opposed. Despite Malthus and Marx, there is at present little evidence to show that starving Swiss and Swedish masses shuffle about in rags.

An Evil to Defeat: Unemployment

Yet Darwin recognized that "if the misery of the poor be caused not by the laws of nature, but by our institutions, great is our sin."[2] Malthus, as also but much later Maynard Keynes, said what has lately become quite evident: that flows of savings do not of themselves ensure flows of investment. Malthus's friend

David Ricardo (1772–1823), another classical economist, believed what has also become quite evident: that (at least in the short and often in the medium term) improved technology displaces workers. "A fixed capital cannot employ all the workers which it is designed to replace." Keynes put the point again in 1936 (he forgot women): "When 9,000,000 men are employed out of 10,000,000 willing and able to work, there is no evidence that the labour of these 9,000,000 men is misdirected. The complaint against the present system is not that these 9,000,000 men ought to be employed on different tasks, but that tasks should be available for the remaining 1,000,000 men."[3] More on this below.

Rationally Unrational: Economic Rationality

Economics hovers between applied science and analytical sociology. It makes the major assumption that markets are acceptably rational and measurable. This is questioned even by some economists.[4] Can the value of love, a wit once asked, be measured by the price of prostitution?

We speak of the rationality of economic man; but we scarcely know on what foundation it rests, how it comes about, or where it is tending. In business, is it more rational to attack than to defend? More rational to collude than to compete? Is it more rational to exchange the untested comforts of the future for the familiar discomforts of the present?

And then, is it rational to achieve a higher corporate output with a lesser number of employees? Of course. But is it, in national consequence, equally rational and efficient to have large pools of unemployed? Of course? Would not some argue that, perhaps, socialism is more rational than capitalism? Socialists, after all, are free to fancy a good future and (alas) enforce it, whereas a capitalist must not only envisage what the future will bring, but also what competitors may do to frustrate his vision. He must not only guess, but outguess the guesses of competitors.

Americans are "rational." So are the Japanese and the Germans. Why then are their economies different? If American economic rationality is the proper model, then German and Japanese economic rationality is an aberration. And if the economic rationality of the Germans and the Japanese is the proper model, then the American model of economic rationality is the aberration.

The Many National Varieties of Capitalism

It is illusory to expect capitalism – a system which is rooted in history and which needs a sprinkling of tolerance to make it work – to be homogeneous in every country. One must look at the meaning of "national" models of different economies. Nationalization of industries is not characteristic of either America, Germany, or Japan. But there is another "social"-ization. It follows from an implied national consensus concerning proper conduct (including proper economic conduct) which prevails in Germany and Japan. Broadly, in "free-form" countries such as the USA and Britain the conduct of corporations is bounded by laws and superficial conventions; in Germany and Japan it is bounded by laws and deep conventions. For purposes of order a "social" or communitarian mentality is as good as any "state ownership of the means of production, distribution and exchange" – or better, because no public coercion is involved. By this I do not mean that the economic system of the Germans and the Japanese is a socialist system, but only that it is also a system.

In 1991 Michel Albert, in *Capitalisme contre capitalisme*, argued that "Rhenish" capital differed from American capitalism in that the former is more consensual, the latter more conflictual. It is not my experience that American business is more conflictual than that of other countries. At standardization and technical development conferences there I found the opposite to be true. I will not argue the case here, but only grant that consensus in the United States and other English-speaking countries is more deliberate and less embedded than in Japan and Germany.

The price paid for such a national consensus is a deferment of the expectations of individuals. Germans, Dutch, Swiss and others, pay this initial price by their acceptance of a general (rather than only in-company) apprenticeship system. For years, apprentices must serve cheaply so as to offer their services more dearly later when they are masters of their trade. Germany, for example, has retained about 260 different apprenticeships by consensus. In Switzerland no electrician or plumber may legally practice his craft without certification, which is why Swiss electricians and plumbers are reliable. In consequence, the *average* level of craft skills is higher in transalpine European countries than countries like Britain and the United States.

From the 19th century into the 20th, incidentally, the industrial revolution brought another distinction: a sharp division between the unskilled and the highly skilled. The factory system created industrial drudges who needed no apprenticeship: jobs could be learnt in hours. But schools had to be founded for administrators, mining engineers, bridge builders and staff officers. They were sent to *grandes écoles* and military academies at West Point, St Cyr and Sandhurst. The industrial revolution both upgraded mankind and downgraded it. More of it went under than went up, and of the ups many swelled the middle classes.

In Japan, every man (rarely any woman) who joins a large *keiretsu* corporation becomes an in-house apprentice of his company. His individual expectations are deferred; his consent to this deferment is mandatory. Whatever his merit, he must climb the same graduated ladder to its higher rungs. He palliates the absence of immediate rewards by the knowledge that he is a qualified cadet in the elite of management. I have for many years repeatedly been told that this is changing, and that merit will henceforth find faster advancement in Japan; but so far the general rule has remained substantially unchanged for any but the highest ranks.

Capitalism Has Many Varieties of Collectivity

In Anglo-Saxon countries, individualism had continually to invent new modes of group endeavor, whereas consciously or subconsciously "Rhenish" and Asian minds held fast to old collective attitudes. (The sense of collectivity in an advanced country can be measured by dividing the Gross Domestic Product by the number of lawyers: the higher the result, the greater is national consensus. Japan wins in this test.) But what is to happen when the old Rhenish model no longer fits new purposes? What if the traditions of their collective capitalism have to change? Does it then follow that Anglo-American individualism will supersede it and become the new inheritor? Will a new form of social tolerance be able to supplant the old successfully? The painful example of East German fusion with the West German model comes to mind; so does the breakdown of the Soviet empire; so does China, twitching between the blanket of communism and wakening restlessness. French and Italians are more fortunate: so far as individualism versus community goes, they have a foot in both traditions. The wrench may be less comfortable for Germans and for Japanese, because, although their mode of life has created settled order, a change of order may discompose their settled life.

To be civilized is to have regard for neighbors. Why then has the West, even Germany, had so many difficulties with collective institutions? Why did it continually have to invent new modes of group endeavor? European collectives – guilds, orders, monasteries, city states, chartered corporations, workers' unions – were driven by purposes. They were in the nature of purposive elites – modes of becoming; while Far Eastern groupings were part of a continuous order of established classes or castes – modes of being.

But why, despite invasions and destructions, did China and India have more continuity of social tenor of civilization and agriculture, than Europe? One supposition is that, in Asia, time repaired and healed: "The invasions, which in the West involved breaks with the past and the birth of new civilizations, were material disasters for China and India, but changed neither their ways of thinking nor their social structures and way of life. There was never a great leap forward like that which took ancient civilization from Greece to Rome, or converted Rome to Christianity...."[5]

One factor which made for Asian permanence may have been the constant need to maintain irrigation systems for the cultivation of rice. In China, Japan, the Plain of the Ganges, in Java and the Philippines, these systems, essential for survival, could not have been preserved except through lasting social disciplines.

In the West, by contrast, there was no respite and no settling down. Instead, in the last two thousand years, one cultural discontinuity replaced another. In addition to the great leaps forward from Greece to Rome and from Rome to Christianity, there was the decline of the Roman empire, the incursions of Goths, Vandals and other "barbarians," the separation of Byzance from Western Christianity. There were changes of mentality: for example, the concept of hell, which in ancient Greece and Rome had been a stagnant place of cold obscurity, was in Christianity transformed into an energetic place of flaming pain and torment. There were great migrations of entire peoples attended by linguistic confusions and diversifications in the early and middle Middle Ages. A darkness and a loss of trade befell Europe when she lost control of the Mediterranean Sea to the Arabs. Feudalism and its structure were dominant for a time, with land the only valuable asset. Costly but mostly vain crusades were launched by the flower of European knighthood.

But Aristotle was rediscovered via Moorish Spain; city states arose in Italy; the arts flowered in the Renaissance; secularization began; trade revived; an encroachment of mercantile practices on the anti-usury teachings of the Church happened. Gradually merchants shook off the dominations of minor feudal lords. For a time, the Church itself divided into two papacies – one in Rome, the other in Southern France. Professional salesmen, quaestors, started to peddle the forgiveness of sins and sold indulgences.

This ultimately led to a further schism – the Reformation – at a time when Northern Europe grew in importance, when the purpose of colonies became aggrandizement, and their peoples became less people than a natural resource for Frenchmen, Englishmen and Spaniards; at a time when the Americas were discovered and gold and silver was raped from them for the greater glory of kings, by adventurers, soldiers and merchants serving Mammon in the name of Christ. Mercantilism – the adoration of gold – ruled for a time; kings compelled wars on land and sea against each other. Capitalism and industry grew; the mass-production of industrial products began by once water-driven, then steam-driven machines. Slaves became superfluous. The Enlightenment burgeoned in France. The power of kings began to decline. Their "divine rights" were first diminished, then curtailed, by the guillotines of France, by the infections of democracy in North America, by the growth of nationalism, by the growth of populations, by the conscience of reformers, by the rationality of science, and by workers' movements of the 19th and 20th centuries which bred new politics as well as democratic and anti-democratic thrusts.

It would be satisfactory to be able to find a common thread and common theme amid this turbulence. Could it be maintained, for example, that throughout, there was a European struggle for liberty and humanism? Even this cannot be maintained with certainty. The term Europe was rare, and was first used politically in the 10th century when Charlemagne's empire was identified only as "Europe, otherwise Charles's Kingdom." Liberty, as a term meaning general freedom, came much later; until the 18th century groups and classes had fought for liberties, but this mainly meant that they were fighting for special affirmations of their privileges. The term Humanism, which in its present meaning signifies the noble independency of man, only dates back to the early 19th century. It had, of course, been used before – from ancient Greece and Rome to the Renaissance – but then mainly meant the nobility of *learning*. In any case, one must be careful with the term: humanism includes such versions of it as Machiavelli's political cynicism, the French Revolution, and existentialism.

One major conclusion may be drawn from this brief account. Unlike the continuities of Eastern cultures despite events, the constant *cultural* discontinuities of Western civilization have accustomed it to change. A readiness to change marks capitalism and corporate development. More than anything else, this is what characterizes the vigor and globality of the modern business system.

Capitalism is an accommodating system. Seen through the prisms of national cultures, the white light of its uniformity is broken into many colors. Its global varieties – those of Europe in particular – are astounding. European civilization and its capitalism may or may not have been the best which has evolved, but it is clearly the most complex.

Economic Simplifications

"Much as contemporary physical scientists are being forced to face up," in Ilya Prigogine's words, to "instability, mutation, and diversification where irreversible processes are constantly at work...," so also the economist "is confronted with 'organic growth' in all its complexity."[6] The complex influence of the Reformation, another economist remarked, while it made not the slightest difference to the force of gravity, may have profoundly changed the demand for fish on Fridays. (It was also one of the causes of the Thirty Years (religious) War.)

Economic causes and their consequences can be direct; they can also be startling. Reasonably predictable consequences are followed by the unpredictable consequences of consequences. A physical scientist would put it differently: he would say that the economy is "algorithmically incompressible." By this he would mean that any accurate model of the economy would have to be as full and intricate as the economy itself. In other words, *such a model would be the economy itself.* An abbreviated model would be unable to include Charles Darwin's "unknown elements of a distinct act of creation."

And therefore economics has to generalize, to average, to simplify. It has to simplify the nature of the market; and what is worse, it has to simplify human nature. It has to abandon the whole man and to replace him by "economic man" and a standard corporation. But no model of the economy can forecast tribal sentiment, nationalism, charity, self-denial, or tolerance. The discordance between Adam Smith's conviction that the selfishness of each leads to the welfare of all, and the commandment to love one's neighbor as oneself, demands not so much love as tolerance. The Japanese economy, for example, works on the assumption that it is the selfishness not of each but of all together which is efficient, and that love has little to do with neighborliness.

We expect the steady flame of certainty even though we know that it flickers. The economist Kenneth Arrow illustrates this by a story from World War II, when some of his colleagues were responsible for the preparation of the following month's long-range weather forecast for the American army. Statisticians found that these forecasts in no way differed from chance. The forecasters themselves were convinced, and asked that the forecasts be discontinued. The army's reply read approximately thus: "the Commanding General, while well aware that the forecasts are no good, nevertheless needs them for planning purposes."[7]

The Unpredictability of "Economic Man" Does not Mean Chaos

The question that arises from this is whether competition is a source of order or a source of disorder.

As mentioned, the economics of capitalism is not computable because an algorithm concerning it would be as extensive, incompressible and non-recurrent as the very system it wishes to compute. It is also certain that, for a time, capitalism is sensitive to the "initial conditions" described in theories of chaos, e.g. the causal fluttering of the wings of an Amazonas butterfly one hundred years ago. But though sensitive to initial conditions, and though complex, incomputable, non-linear and imperfectly predictable, the self-corrective business system has yet lately proved to be reasonably non-chaotic. The watchdogs of the Ethos of Conviction – socio-political institutions, society and the media – as well as the business watchdogs of the Ethos of Success – competitive analysis, competition itself, the inclination of business to set temporary limits to commercial attritions – have not let it descend again to the uncontrolled disorders of the 1920s and 1930s.

Nor will future watchdogs let it do so in any civilized society inhabited by corporations with a civilized intent. Capitalism itself, and the societies in which it operates, have gained in complexity and reach, and will continue to do so. It is not therefore sensible to hope for a shrunken "minimum state." To shrink, *a "minimum state" would need a minimum capitalism.* Even the minimum state's keenest defenders would jib at such a ruinous reduction.

Capitalism and business will continue to grow; and with it society's demands for supervised and social purposes. States may find ways to reduce the number of people they employ; but are unlikely to surrender the powers they command. Within such limits as it must impose on itself, *laissez-faire* business is possible; but *laissez-faire* government is a contradiction in terms. Government may, indeed should, be disposed to let business use its lawful vigor and initiatives; but it is a neglect of duty not to keep under careful review that which democratic government has permitted.

If competition were only a form of battle then victory for one side, and surrender by the other, would mean victory for the monopoly of the victor. It would bring order, but not desirable order. Such is not the case: that which makes competition work as a social mechanism is not the pitched battle but the voluntary truce. Competition is a form of compromise. Almost every act in business is a reconciliation of warring probabilities. French often uses the word *tâtonnement* for bargaining: the word means groping, feeling one's way, adjusting.

On the credit side I note that business suitably fits into the culture of liberal democracy – not because the two are identical, but because they are complementary. Business needs peace, not wars. Business seeks wealth, not internal justice. For its part, liberal democracy must seek a degree of justice and social fairness. Unfortunately, fairness and justice are not in the business of making money. But since both business and democracy use compromise and tolerance as means, a complementarity of partial opposites emerges. *Competition is as much about the containment of power as it is about the determination of prices.* It is this ability to contain power by competition that makes modern capitalism acceptable to democracy.

Capitalism Works When it Inclines to Tolerance

Corporations teeter between the desire for market advantage and fear of competitors' retaliation. In the short run, market share and price stability is the only safe strategy. That is a rule of the game. But sooner or later corporations must seek an advantage which cannot be quickly copied. That also is a rule of the game. In the long run change is the only safe strategy. An example of this is the many cross-border alliances, joint ventures and cooperative agreements formed between corporations of one country with those of another (which in fact constitute a larger sector of the global economy than international mergers and acquisitions). They are made in the interests both of temporary stability *and* of pending change. It may be argued that these compacts between participating corporations are a management of trade. They are indeed a management of trade; but they are often management by enlargement rather than by restriction.

A warning before we go to competition as a temporary form of tolerance: "Change" is the fashionable savior. Sermons are daily preached to people in business enjoining them to learn to change themselves and change their corporation's governance and conduct. But, unlike at times America or Britain, Germany, for one, will not sacrifice a strong base of monetary stability for any tempting changes. Changes must indeed be met or made; but changes must begin from balance; they must end there, too.

The Japanese have a considered way of meeting change. The reason why it usually takes some time to strike a deal in Japan is that the Japanese do not start with "Where do we want to get to?" but with "Where are we now?" If where they are fits well with where they could be going, the deal is struck; if not, not. They start with the recognition of stability. *Destination follows from location.*

An opposite example is Britain. After World War II,

believing that the social consequences of private enterprise were baleful, it nationalized enterprises. Under a following government this was reversed: it tried aggressive continuity. This did not take, either. The next government turned to faith in technology. This vaccination also did not take. Then, under Mrs Thatcher, all social ills were to be cured in an adored, celestial market place. Britain's problem now is not that business fails to see the need for change, but that it does not know its starting points. Nor are such British institutions as the banks acclimatized to the financial needs of change and to approaches to risk and venture capital. Britain has many stabilities; but some of its stabilities still fail to favor investment and new technology.

Tolerance: or the Domestication of the Absolute

Tolerance has been a late acquisition of the West. Democracy and the business system would fail without it.

Tolerance is new. Until approximately the beginning of the 18th century the word *tolérance* was, in French usage, a term of condemnation. Toleration was nothing but "a lax complacency towards evil." In 1691, in an admonition to Protestants, Bossuet, Bishop of Meaux, though he opposed the killing of Protestants, still proudly described Catholicism as the least tolerant of all religions.[8]

Not only Catholics. Here are the words of James Ussher, Irish Protestant Archbishop of Armagh, on Catholics, in 1626: "to give them ... toleration, ... that they may freely exercise their religion ... is a grievous sin."

An historian[9] writing in 1973 tells us that at about the same time, and as if to compete with Bossuet's boast, the Protestant Synod of Leyden, an overwhelming majority of whose members were Huguenot refugees from Catholic persecution, firmly condemned religious toleration as a heresy. Only recently, she says, has a Jesuit been able to enter Sweden. Theoretically if not actually, Switzerland is still closed to him. This is no doubt better than the first form of intolerance, that of Charlemagne against the Saxons, who were given the choice between baptism and death, a recipe later adopted by the Spanish Inquisition.

Nor are Muslims exempt. An apocryphal story whose logic is still approved by some fundamentalists today (whether Christian, Muslim or Jewish) tells of Alexandria at the time of its conquest in AD 640 by Emir Amrou. He asked the Caliph Omar what should be done to the great Alexandria Library and its great riches of classical Greek and Roman scrolls. Omar ruled that the contents were either contrary to the Koran and were therefore to be destroyed, or they accorded with the Koran, and were therefore to be destroyed because superfluous. Accordingly, all the contents of the library were torched.

Many centuries later, towards the end of the 18th century, the idea of civil and religious toleration entered the conscience even of absolute and "enlightened" despots, such as Joseph II, heir to the Hapsburg throne, and son of Maria Theresa, Empress of Austria. She warned him that toleration and indifferentism were a carelessness about religious truth that would damage or destroy it. He answered her by saying that toleration certainly did not mean religious indifference. But as far as he was concerned toleration in temporal matters meant that he would employ anyone without regard to his religion. He would allow him to be a full citizen, own property and follow a profession, so long as he was a fit person capable of useful service to the state. He lived up to his promise as well as he could: between 1781 and 1786 he issued a new and "universal" civil code of law, an Edict of Toleration, abolished serfdom, abolished torture, abolished most of the disabilities of the Jews, abolished the penalty of death, let the press be reasonably free (but balked at the idea of political democracy).

Free Enterprise Demands Tolerance

What is tolerance? It is certainly not indifference. To tolerate is to dislike but bear: "To tolerate is first to condemn and then put up with...."[10]

Tolerance is a confinement of dogma. A faith – whether communism, Christianity or religious fundamentalism – which claims to be the One Eternal Truth or the One Universal Salvation, is apt to incline to intolerance. It reasons that it is quite intolerable that the One Truth should have to share the world with any other. To the One Truth other "truths" seem not only lies, but intolerable lies. And even a "truth" which professes toleration may regard a rival truth, which does not profess it, to be damnable heresy and intolerable error. One who says that he loves mankind, but believes that there is no salvation outside the church, feels bidden to usher people into the Church That Saves – and summon them by force if necessary.

Then there is a paradox of tolerance: those who love liberty and tolerance cannot, beyond a limit, bend to an adversary who has the will and the power to abolish liberty and tolerance. As in most matters of human coexistence, tolerance is a matter of degree: the more reasonable the society, the higher its threshold of forbearance. Absolute "principle," on the other hand, is quirky and commanding. It wears the stiff armor of dogma, and insists that this is more comfortable than the loose robe of tolerance.

Even so unbigoted a man as John Locke held (in 1688, in *A Letter Concerning Toleration*) that certain views and deeds were not to be suffered. Among these were opinions contrary to "those moral rules necessary for the preservation of civil society:" claims to extraordinary privilege; attempts to seize government; attempts to seize the property of citizens; also treason; but also atheism. An atheist should be excluded from toleration since one who denies God cannot truly swear a sacred oath; a Roman Catholic, too, since he owes allegiance to a prince at Rome and cannot therefore swear full and true allegiance to a British king. In this respect the English Whig John Locke lagged behind his French Huguenot contemporary Pierre Bayle, who (in 1682, in *Pensées sur la comète*) argued that moral integrity was not dependent on religion.

It is, at any rate, approximately with Bayle and Locke that the Western idea of civil tolerance and religious toleration turned from being one of civilization's delicate fruits to being one of its strong roots.

It should by now be evident that free enterprise and free trade are forms of conduct inseparable from a high degree of tolerance.

Summary

Capitalism is aggressive, competitive, bellicose, dynamic, unforgiving, unrelenting and hardheaded.

So it is said by some of its defenders and many of its accusers. Even though it added to the wealth of nations, would it have been accepted in this, its hard, dogmatic form?

Not only would it be unaccepted in this Darwinian mold, it would not even work in it. Fortunately for itself and everyone, its jagged edges are blunted by competition, by the conventions and cultures of nations, and by the social controls and countervailing actions of democratic parliaments and governments; above all, by its own disposition for considered advances, timely retreats, compromise and – tolerance.

10

Competition:
The Reformation of the
Business System

The gradual enforcement of business competition was an American metamorphosis of Adam Smith's Scottish Enlightenment ideas. Despite its avowal of free enterprise, America decided against a freedom for commerce and industry to carve the fatted calf in any way it chose. In this century, anti-trust measures in the United States assumed a stern and unrelenting reign.

The mentality of mercantilism, colonization, collusion and monopoly were still the norm in European countries at the time when the Americans cut their ties to the English crown. It was only after

World War II that Europe – somewhat shamefacedly – surrendered to the dominance of American anti-trust and anti-monopoly morality and its enforcements. Yet collusiveness and "arranged markets" continued covertly in Europe and Japan, and this mentality continues to have adherents and practitioners.

By coincidence the second half of the 20th century has also seen the greatest burgeoning of wealth. Neither I, nor anyone, can prove a direct causal connection between lively competition and rising wealth. But in this case, I and many others willingly accept an "after it, therefore because of it."

Competition rarely kills those with open eyes. What kills is myopia. What also kills is the kind of corporate ambition which swaps a proper balance of assets and liabilities for one gigantic corporate debt.

And so, none in business likes competition; and so, all in business like it.

Competition: The Reformation of the Business System

Restraint of Trade: the Way to Failure

Stalin's most fateful mistake was made in 1924. He proclaimed the doctrine of "Socialism in One Country" and closed the borders of the Soviet Union hermetically for absolute political control. Foreign trade was limited to just the amount necessary to buy materials and resources not available inside the Soviet Union. The main economic effect of the measure was to abolish international competition. And so, by degrees, Soviet prices and costs became divorced from prices and costs in the rest of the world. Distortion reached a point at which, in the 1980s, the Soviet Union could produce many of the same goods as the West, including military and "space" equipment, but at several times Western cost, and mostly of inferior quality. The Soviet Union became a "planned" economy which only planned its inefficiencies.

There were many similar tendencies in the West. They did not aim at "socialism in one country." They aimed at protectionism, which is capitalism by exclusion. Like the "As Is" agreement whose story follows, they aimed at global monopoly in one industry. The examples below illustrate the view that the capitalism of the late 19th and the first half of the 20th century was not the capitalism of the late 20th century either in thought or, with exceptions, in deed. Collusion was then a common form of managed trade – collusion which was either legal, or illegal but unpunished. That it is now mostly culpable may demonstrate some moral progress. It may also show that such progress has been impressed on Europe by the official doctrines of the United States. The transition was gradual. Events after World War II show that the old mentality persisted, and continues to persist in many countries.

Restraint of Trade: a Way to Success?

The Organization of Petroleum-Exporting Countries, OPEC, was founded in the early 1970s. It angered the world by its monopolizing, and by the many hardships it inflicted on poorer countries.

Yet it was nothing new. Consider the almost forgotten history of the "Achnacarry Agreement," critically told by Anthony Sampson in 1975,[1] and earlier, less critically, by Adolf Berle in 1955.[2] Berle's description was largely based on reports by the Federal Trade Commission and the Department of Justice of the United States. "Anti-trust legalistics aside, the story is amazing and far from any picture of crime."

Nothing wrong, indeed? I set a short part of it down as he presented it with the full flavor of contemporaneousness, and ask what his then indulgent judgment might have been today. I suppose that whether one is for or against what happened depends on whose ox was gored. But let the reader be the judge of this agreement which was more precise, detailed, and comprehensive than any agreement signed between members of the oil-producing countries, OPEC.

The story as told by Berle, "in salient outline," and shortened or annotated (where marked []), starts like this:

"In the year 1926 a relative balance of power existed in the world's oil markets. It had been reached by a complex series of bilateral and multilateral agreements between the world's large oil companies in respect of various oilfields. Geographically these extended all the way from the Dutch East Indies and Iran to Venezuela and Bolivia. Seven companies had an overwhelming majority of world production: Royal Dutch Shell, Anglo-Persian, Standard Oil of New Jersey, Socony-Vacuum (now Mobil), Gulf, Texas, Atlantic Refining Company. The balance was uneasy. [] They were in dubious equilibrium in 1926 when a commercial conflict broke out in India.

"There, Socony-Vacuum Oil Company had purchased Russian oil from wells previously belonging to Royal Dutch Shell, but later nationalized by the Soviet government. Shell, belonging to British and Dutch interests, resented this; in any event, a price war broke out between Socony and Shell in the Indian market. Shell presently extended the war to the United States, directly invading the American market. Socony promptly counter-attacked by entering the British market, and competition and price war thus became general.

"At this point the more responsible brains in the oil industry went to work on the situation, with the result that in September 1928 a conference was held at Achnacarry House in Scotland, the home of Sir Henri Deterding, head of Shell. It is reported that the heads of the Standard Oil of New Jersey, Shell, and Anglo-Persian (later BP) oil companies were the negotiators. The result was a document [] later referred to as the 'Achnacarry Agreement,' or by the more descriptive name of the 'As Is' Agreement. It was, in effect, a treaty of commercial peace concluding an economic war between great corporations. As the war had become world-wide, the peace necessarily had to deal with world conditions in the oil industry. It established what may be described, without too much exaggeration, as *the most successful experiment in economic world government thus far achieved in the twentieth century.* [Present author's emphasis.]

"Summarized, the 'As Is' Agreement adopted seven governing principles. (1) Each company was to retain the [*status quo ante* share] of the market, everywhere, enjoyed at the time by that company. [] (2) The existing facilities of all companies were to be made available to competitors [] at a cost not less than any company would incur if it built new facilities. (3) New facilities were to be built only to supply increased consumption requirements. (4) Each producing area should sell in the nearest market [to it]. (5) Supplies for each market should be drawn from the nearest producing area. (6) Surplus production in any producing area was not to be 'dumped' in other areas to the disturbance of the price structure there prevailing. In practice this meant that surplus production could be sold anywhere at the prevailing price – but if it could not be sold at that price must be shut in. (7) No measures were to be taken which would materially increase the cost of producing oil.

"The domestic market and import trade of the United States was exempted from this arrangement, lest the companies agreeing to it find themselves in conflict with the Sherman anti-trust law [of 1890, which forbade 'combination of conspiracy in restraint of trade']; but apparently the American companies hoped to use the Webb-Pomerene Act [of 1918, which eased anti-trust rules for exporters] and the conservation principles [known as 'rules of reason'] which later emerged in American domestic legislation so as to give substantial effect to the 'As Is' principles."

Berle then describes the details of this intricate web after 1928 and says: "[a]n evaluation of this really remarkable and pragmatically successful experiment in planned economy is difficult to make. The attitudes of different people are completely opposed. To the European mentality, perhaps especially to the British, arrangements of this sort represent ordinary common sense: by their criteria the results were brilliant. To American doctrine at the very least they represent danger, and very possibly criminal restraint of trade. [] The [US] Department of

Justice among other things attempted to subpoena the records of the Anglo-Iranian Oil Company. At this point the British Government promptly objected on the ground that this was a British company, and that British records were not subject to the jurisdiction of American courts."

Berle surmises: "The fact was that from 1928 to 1939, the period in which the Achnacarry Agreement and its successor arrangements governed the petroleum supplies of the world, there was peace, and there was production, and there was distribution, and there was stable and reasonably acceptable price. By absolute standards, the Agreement has to be accounted a success. Plenty of peace treaties have had a worse fate. Criticism would have to be based on hypothetical comparison between the actual results and those which might have been attained. Obviously the major oil companies did not lose by the Achnacarry arrangements, but then there is little virtue to be found in a losing operation."[] "But if we are indulging in 'might-have-beens', there is no solid reason to assume that unrestricted world competition would have produced more satisfactory results."[] "As an experiment in world economic government [Berle concludes] the corporations cannot on this record be accused of failure."

But they can. Had it occurred to the oil company members of the Achnacarry Agreement to offer a shareholding in themselves to the source countries, many subsequent wars and disagreement would probably not have arisen. They would have pitched their tents together, and dwelt in them. As it turned out in the years after World War II, these countries awoke to their rights of sovereignty and disinherited the oil corporations of the West.

Other, similar, and no less powerful agreements in restraint and control of trade were common before World War II. One of these was the inorganic chemicals cartel controlled by Ernest Solvay (see Chapter 1). Cartelization, now immoral and illegal, was moral and legal in Europe not long ago. One major surviving cartel, now possibly endangered, continues in the diamond industry.

Three Personal Experiences of Anti-Competitive Behavior

In the early 1950s I became involved in the steel pipe business. There then existed a conference of European steel mills, complete with a well-known international accountancy firm to keep its records, which regularly met to allocate quotas and fix minimum prices. It was one of the oldest, if not the oldest, producers' agreements in control of trade. Its origins went back to the turn of the century, and it continued by fits and starts from quick break-downs to slow reconstitutions. Even Japanese mills attended from time to time. American mills refrained. Breaches of agreements being more common than their observance, it never worked as well as that described by Berle, but not for want of perseverance. It ended in the late 1970s when German mills became aware that their government was about to mount an investigation.

The other example is the system, known as "channelling," used by Japanese steel pipe mills. The starting condition is that every producing mill has at least one, usually two, preferred Japanese international trading companies who vigorosly seek out customers for it throughout the world. A battle ensues between the mills-plus-their-traders for *new* business from that client. The battle is in earnest: the mills vie for acceptance by the customer on price. Prices fall until one or other mill-plus-trader secures the order. Thereafter, peace is for a while restored. The mill, its trader and the client are then registered as one unit of "property." No other mill bids against the registered mill. The defeated mill will not, of course, refuse to make an offer to that customer if so requested. But it will not outbid the channelled mill. In return, other customers will be the respected "property" of other channels.

When markets are depressed, the Ministry of International Trade and Industry, MITI, will suggest or allow a "depression cartel" whereby mills reduce production by an agreed percentage and, in the case of massive orders, allow several mills to share production. The system, as any other for "orderly marketing," is more complicated than here described. But this is the system in broad outline. It is not one of which the Japanese bothered to make too great a secret.

Something befell me in the middle 1960s. I had been hired by a British manufacturer to run a marketing operation in Germany. My task was to capture three or so percent of the domestic German market for certain industrial products and components within about a year. Offices were leased and salesmen engaged. Within a year, duty had been done. One day, two senior managers of the parent manufacturer arrived, and announced that the effort would be terminated – not for lack of performance but, on the contrary, for its achievement. It then emerged that the exercise had been launched to teach the German competition a lesson: "You have tried to enter the British market. Cease." The lesson having been taught, further efforts were not needed. The German competitors had agreed to withdraw from the British market. I had not, of course, been told that my fellow workers and I were to be patsies. Here, in Anthony Sampson's words, "competing one moment and conniving the next," was one way of using competition to oust competition.

No fair-minded state should today permit a business system to continue indefinitely without domestic competition, or, in the case of utilities, without constraints. Governments, however, with the ancient inertia of patriotic zeal, still try to protect "domestic" corporations against foreign competition – shamefacedly sometimes, blatantly at others. Reciprocal airlines' landing rights are an example.

While one shop is monopoly and two shops are competition, three shops are a market. Only competition makes markets acceptable as social institutions. Competition is not a problem for business alone, but far more a problem for governments. Business competition creates a new topography for governments, states, laws, and political parties. *As long as government insists that business engage in competition it must put up with the fact that competition will change the nature and the task of government.*

Tolerance Of Competition Is Not From Love But From Necessity

Tolerance of competition is less a test of business democracy than a test of its virility. Religious and political systems may or may not be tolerant; they may or may not survive without tolerance; but a high degree of tolerance must be integral to the business system. I shall leave aside the difference between tolerance because you want to be tolerant, and tolerance because you have to be tolerant. With a touch of hypocrisy to help it along, the one becomes the other. But tolerance is not indifference: I have seen businesses become too dispassionate about competition and have seen them become too mechanical to withstand it.

Business often competes by what may be called a "one percent monopoly;" which is the name I gave to the circumstance that when I tried to get an order it was enough – other things being equal – to be just one percent or so better than my competitors. (In the case of one major order it was one-eighth of one percent.) The other ninety-nine or so percent were common to us all. I have since discovered that this is much the same principle as Gauze's Hypothesis or the Principle of Competitive Exclusion in nature: competition between closely related species tends, little by little, to effect a separation of these species. Under a given set of conditions one survives, the other expires.

Tolerance of competitors in business is not from love for them. I have yet to meet a fighting cock of business who would not rather rule the roost alone. Like many business people, I had no love of competition, no love of the mortar and pestle of price, the hammer and anvil of delivery times, the cleaver and block of payment terms and supplier's credits. But I must agree that when I had competition, it did considerably sharpen my pugnacity. Henry Ford said (though later in life himself forgot) that "business is never as healthy as when, like a chicken, it must do a certain amount of scratching for what it gets."[3]

Still, why is the "normal" competitive poise of businesses oligopolistic, with no conspirators yet a conspiracy of sorts? Corporations tend not to undercut but match: one company's price list looks much like another's for the same product or service. Price tends to match price. Furtively offered discounts are more frequent than open war. We know that price congruence does not last, and that some corporation will break out to challenge another – which usually happens when a cluster of new (real or merely persuasive) benefits is added to differentiate the product.

And yet, why is pricing oligopolistic for much of the time? The answer lies somewhere in game theory and a phenomenon well-known as the "prisoner's dilemma:" two prisoners are interrogated; if neither confesses, each will serve one year in prison; if both confess, they serve five years each; if one confesses, he goes free while the other receives a ten-year sentence. Therefore the rational decision is to be silent, because the silences of oligopoly bring interim stability. There are few other ways to explain their ancient and universal use in business. Price is the signal a company sends to another when it is not sending any other. But price hides cost; and cost, not price, hones the edge that cuts one's rivals.

"Inside Information" Has Its Good Sides

Damned if you do, damned if you don't: a note on "insider dealing." The concept is too ambivalent, far too open to legal interpretation. Best known is the pursuit by regulators of insider dealing in the securities industry.

But normal manufacturing and trading runs on "inside" information. Not to gather such knowledge, not to be abreast of the details of the market, is to condemn oneself for failure to do one's duty to the corporation and to those who depend on it. It is not possible to be a good businessman or businesswoman unless one is, in full understanding, well "inside" one's own and one's competitors' business. "Insider"-ness is professional as long as it is reached by painstaking observation and not by outright spying or collusion. One can learn astoundingly well what competitors intend by looking through the windows of careful competitive analysis. One may by this means come to know more about them than they know themselves – which then is hardly spying. Competitive analysis yields a better and more continuous view than glances through forbidden keyholes. Governments that preach a market philosophy but employ spies to gather industrial intelligence waste taxpayers' money. Technology and product licenses are cheaper and better. In addition to knowledge they buy continuous advice.

"Insider"-ness is asking questions all the time. Nothing about it is culpable. If such activity were to be officially enjoined from an excess of legal conscience, business would slow, markets would become "imperfect," or would be made as inefficient as they were in communist countries in which all commercial information, including costs and prices, was turned into a well-guarded secret of the state.

An example: In the early 1970s, I bought most of my supplies of oil and gas-well pipe for the South-East Asian market from an American steel mill. Its prices at the time were on the bare edge of competitiveness, but any excess of price was balanced by a good reputation for quality, especially for high-grade pipe. One day, when I visited this steel corporation in the USA, I was told that, in their view, their prices for the higher grades were too low. They based this argument on the theory that because they had the highest reputation, no oil company would risk using pipe for demanding service made by other nations. These other nations would be left to sell low grades, with high grades remaining the sole preserve of American mills. They therefore intended to charge higher prices for premium grades of pipe. This did not presage well for my business. I had to prepare to buy from other mills in other countries.

In due course, the American mill did increase its price differentials to levels justified only by high hopes. Foreign mills, particularly the Japanese, attracted by the new high premiums, doubled their efforts to sell high-grade pipe, and in due course succeeded. Five years later American mills were left with an unprofitable aristocracy of price.

My preparations were by that time complete and were to my advantage. Was this a use of illicit insider information or was it simple prudence? Prudence, I say.

I look back from the middle 1990s to the early 1970s: it took American mills some twenty years to retreat from unintended suicide. There are mills in the USA and Canada today as competitive as any in the world, and more competitive than many Japanese mills. There are, of course, far fewer of them. Many died unkilled; they killed themselves by misconception. Pricing is not a tactical maneuver. If it is based on real ability, price is the final, published expression of strategic intention. It reaches deep into the bowels of cost.

For Planning Use Capitalism. It Has More Of It Than Communism

On one occasion in Moscow in the late 1970s I gossiped with a buyer in a large Soviet government import and export corporation. There was, I goaded, not enough planning in the Soviet Union. There was more planning in capitalist than in communist countries: witness the proliferation of computers in every Western company and their relative scarcity in the Soviet Union. Was not the computer a tool for manifesting ordered patterns from a mass of data? And did not the grand planning of the Soviet Union leave far too much unplanned to cope with the vagaries of nature and accidental happenings? Was not the Soviet Union's economy a backbone with an insufficient nervous system? His answer then was silence which history later broke.

Summary

Monopoly is sweet, and competition is only an acquired taste. Business people love competition about as much as knives love whetstones.

Competition is a *public* function and is not natural to capitalism. On the face of it, the rules of competition are of benefit to the consumer (a now numerous class new to history); but in so doing they improve production and supply, though not always farsightedness.

As Adam Smith maintained, and as this chapter illustrates, it is best executed by business but designed and enforced by the public.

11

Competition and the Common Purpose

" We can do something for posterity but it can do nothing for us. "
John Rawls (1921-)[1]

" If the misery of the poor be caused not by the laws of nature, but by our institutions, great is our sin. "
Charles Darwin (1809–1882)[2]

" [T]he man whom we naturally love and revere the most, is he who joins, in the most perfect command of his

own ... sympathetic feelings, the most exquisite sensi-
bility ... to the ... sympathetic feelings of others. **"**
Adam Smith (1723–1790)[3]

" Between the idea And the reality Between the motion
And the act Falls the Shadow **"**
T.S. Eliot (1888–1965)[4]

*Chapter 1 argued (as does the rest of the book) that capitalism is not an
ideology but a) a crucial procedure, b) a self-transforming system, c) a
shaper of everyday life, and d) that its "past is a foreign country."
Chapter 2 held that progress is not automatic but is sustained by
science, business and enthusiasm. Chapter 3 said that property rights
are more attempts at some sort of order than at some sort of justice.
Chapters 4 and 5 were on the Janus-face of human nature: the Ethos of
Success versus the Ethos of Conviction. Chapters 6, 7 and 8 asked how
corporate "personhood" fits in with the personhood of individuals and
with the personhood of other corporations – then claimed that tolerance
had much to do with it. Chapters 9 and 10 considered the relationship
between the civil corporation, competition, and tolerance. It regretted
that corporations are unusually mortal, mutating aggregations whose
good intentions are heavily dependent on the ups and downs of quar-
terly balance sheets and profit-and-loss statements. Therefore corporations, singly, are inconstant stakeholders' benefactors.*

*All the concepts treated were usually the outcomes of muddles, but
all went towards the making of the corporate system. We turn to what
corporations could do in future decades to further the civility and
humanism of the business system as a whole.*

Competition and the Common Purpose

" Capitalism prospers best in an environment with a peculiar combination of self-interested behavior – enough to induce individuals to look for profitable activities – and non-self-interested behavior, where one's word is one's honor, where social rather than economic sanctions suffice to enforce contracts. "

Joseph E. Stiglitz, *Wither Socialism?*, MIT Press, Cambridge, MA, 1994, p. 271

The Explored Land

"Management" discovered itself as a serious discipline in the middle 1950s. The business world was then securely swaddled in the Bretton Woods Agreement and in American financial dominance. The task of business education was to make business rational, scientific and humane. A "science" of marketing evolved. Corporations were told to be broadminded. Capitalistic toughmindedness, "Theory X," was to be discarded and capitalistic liberalism, "Theory Y," adopted. Business education encouraged a brave dynamic in a Western world which was progressing democratically and becoming richer.

The *Harvard Business Review* taught smart thinking and

straight dealing. Good corporate conduct, organizationally and ethically, was the theme – more than the wars and attritions of competition. Leaders of American business wrote long and generous essays on *Big Business and Human Values*, on *The Uncommon Man* and on *Business and Social Change*.[5] The welfare state was arriving in the West and stability-with-growth seemed an attainable ideal. The world's economy had a broad and Keynesian sweep and humanism was compatible with business.

The only massively looming peril was communism *versus* the West; but this conflict was hermetically sealed in the geo-political envelope. It had little relevance to trade and to the economic conduct of Western business and its corporations. The Orient was inconsiderable and unconsidered.

Since then – from about the middle 1970s – business schools have taught narrower doctrines and techniques. Until recently, recommended conduct yielded to a number of recommended procedures.

Meanwhile, in the "real" world, corporations tried a startlingly large number of procedures.

Corporations increased their size by organic growth, by acquisition, by mergers, by conglomeration, by leveraged buy-outs, by management buy-outs. They decreased their size by de-conglomeration, by the sell-off of subsidiaries, by returning to their "core" competences, by downsizing, by breakup. They tried to become more efficient by flattening management structures, reengineering, Total Quality Management, competitive analyses, (economic) value analyses, benchmarking, just-in-time deliveries and inventories. They tried to become more flexible by "externalization:" by "out-sourcing" knowledge, "out-sourcing" supplies, signing temporary contracts of attachment, joint ventures, joint research and development (R&D), and cross-licencing.

These models either worked or failed, but few of them, if any, ring of explicit *social* functionality. Business in the aggregate is a social institution, but in mid-battle each company alone is only capable of a fluctuating benevolence.

All these techniques have been applied in the USA and Britain; few of them have been used in Germany, and fewer still in Japan. All of which demonstrates that capitalism is still an uncertain system, full of experiment and interim solutions.

The Land Beyond

I said elsewhere that business lacks a perspective on coming human generations, can scarcely have it and cannot afford it. Their fate is beyond the grasp of business. How much it might allot to the debt between the present and coming generations is beyond the calculus of any "social rate of discount." The duties of care which are common to families and communities are almost beyond the corporation. (Almost, but not quite: a path across the gap is suggested below.)

This is not to say that people in corporations are unconcerned. But it is to say that corporations, however solicitous of stakeholders, cannot put these concerns fully at the core of commercial policies. However ruthful they may be of the fate of those they have had to dismiss from their employment, and however reasonable the settlement they may attempt to strike with them when this happens, no corporation can support the children of its past employed.

No corporation can ensure that children have good and useful schooling even though it itself depends on an educated workforce. Commercial competition is not a device made for familial care. Some may claim that corporations now are ecologically concerned for the health of present and future generations. But even this is due more to the impositions of public policy and social hygiene.

Retraining people for new skills is a moderate solution, but incomplete. What matters as much as training is trainability.

Training for trainability and flexibility of mind must begin in early childhood when the young imagination can take fire.

Corporations do not die in law; in reality their lives are often short. Any social compact they may strike with those who work in them, who contributed their capital, in whose vicinity they have their factories and offices, soon ceases upon hard times, insolvency, or bankruptcy, or liquidation. Mergers, take-overs and buy-outs rarely guarantee that earlier promises of security can be fully kept. The general sociology of corporations, or any social models corporations themselves create, lose their significance when corporations fade. A nation's business, in its entirety, contributes to a nation's wealth but little to its nation-hood. Nor can corporations, except as agents of the nation, secure the rights and liberties of man.

For Example: A Naked Futurology

In the Republic of Eurica, about the year 2000, a populist politician made it his mission to found an "Industrial and Universal Union of the Unemployed against Unemployment,"
IUUUU, generally referred to in speeches as the "I Double-U
Double-U" (thus unwittingly echoing the name of the radical
IWW, the Industrial Workers of the World, or "Wobblies," of
the western United States in the early 20th century).
At that future time the unemployed constituted about fifteen
percent of the voting population – nearly thirty percent when
counted with their wives and other voting members of their
families. Also, in an "age of knowledge," things had been
made worse because much human knowledge and skill had
been delegated to computers, "expert systems" and "artificial
intelligence" machines. Permanent or semi-permanent
unemployment had struck not only "workers," but also
musicians, managers, ex-soldiers and ex-officers, masters of

business administration, tool-and-die makers, and so on. Unemployment was no longer a single class phenomenon. True, more than seventy percent of the population had jobs and enjoyed The Culture of Contentment. They did not seek social change – a quietest phenomenon which by then had become known as The Inertia of Adequate Condition. The politician however reasoned that his thirty percent undoubtedly was the single greatest voting bloc with a single overarching problem.

The I₄U became a dominant political force. Worse, it manifested its discontents by continuous picketing, lobbying, public demonstrations, disruptions of traffic and the passage of goods. The politicians' party adopted a platform convenient to the I₄U. This platform's demand was simple: "Let all technology, all efficiency, all international competitiveness go hang; let them play second fiddle to work, to jobs, to dignity." The other major party, reluctant but fearful of displacement, was forced to adopt a similar platform. There were, certainly, many liberals, conservatives, libertarians and reactionary *status-quo-ante*diluvians who opposed the tendency. Some churches however, among them the Church of Rome, approved it, and quoted the Pope's 1991 encyclical *Centesimus Annus*: "The obligation to earn one's bread by the sweat of one's brow also presumes the right to do so."

But the clamor had grown too loud. In due course the matter became a constitutional issue. A necessary two-thirds majority of territories and members of legislatures voted for a constitutional amendment which read approximately thus: "Full employment being necessary to the life, liberty, and pursuit of happiness of the people, Congress shall make no laws abridging the right to work and opportunities thereto, nor permit any such laws to continue."

In immediate consequence, Eurica withdrew from the World Trade Organization. Similar movements had meanwhile arisen in several other advanced economies of the world. There followed a worldwide retreat from free trade and the flow of international investments. *Et cetera.*

Ten years after the passage of the constitutional amendment the unemployment rate had of course doubled in Eurica and the rest of the world. The leaders of business, the leaders of labor and high intellectuals repeatedly met together to reconcile their points of view and to decide on a platform of common interest to put to government for the solution of the problems of industrial society – problems which by then had become an inextricable mixture of the social, the political and the economic.

They could not agree. They remained divided into countries of freedom and countries of equality. "Countries of freedom" chose a minimally controlled system in which most could find jobs – some with egregious splendors of reward and many more at bare subsistence levels (if that). "Countries of equality" chose a controlled system in which none was excessively rewarded and none pitifully. All were given work or make-work work.

The world remained ununified. Some people were "satisfied;" no one was satisficed. The demands for national pride had been met. Their price was poverty.

The Waning of Ideologies, the Waxing of Cultures

But this is not a book of prophecy. If it were, it would note a reluctant and fragmented return to a recognition of certain "natural" rights of men. As in the *Digest* of the Emperor Justinian in AD 533, these rights extend to "the following things [which] are by natural law common to all – the air, running water, the sea and the shore." The notion of ecology is entirely a notion of natural justice.

If this were a book of prophecy it would note that there is no technical revolution today to compare with electrification, or the telephone, or the building of railways and railroads in the 19th century. There are no "locomotive" technologies today to compare in relative impact, size and scope with these. Though there are more new technologies now than ever, yet the national product has become so immense that even the growth of the computer and biotechnology industries is *relatively* small in its percentage effect on the total economic product of any developed nation. The largest waiting train today is the modernization of nations – such as Japan's since World War II and the rebuilding of Europe in the 1950s – but who will build the tracks and supply motives and locomotives?

If this were a book of prophecy it would record the prophecies of those who, dazzled by the power of the computer, believe that this great tool for automation and information is also an infallible guide to the making of major decisions. Those leaders of business whom I asked how far they could rely on computer dissection to chart the future course of their own corporations, answered precisely that it was good for 20 percent of any decision, or 30 percent at best; and that the other 70 to 80 percent were the usual and accustomed headache. I agree with their assessment. Information, unfortunately, is always and only about the past.

If this were a book of history it would note that ideology is no longer a dominating force. Like ants lost to the antheap, ideologues have become nervous and uncertain: they have random ideals but no ideology to house them. It would note that many human motives are non-economic: pilgrimages to Lourdes, Jerusalem or Mecca, say, may be of enormous economic interest to local shopkeepers, but that is not why people make them. It would note that governments in the 1990s are wary of social and economic experimentation. They prefer to leave experimentation to business, which is, as every business person knows, an experimental system of risky choices.

If this were a book on the ironies of history it would note a remarkable reversal. For over a century and a half, the left – political socialists, Christian socialists, and communists – saw competition as a destructive game played by capitalists – a game that harmed ordinary people and "immiserated" them. Adam Smith was reviled as an advocate of "free" enterprise who saw the exercise of private greed as an acceptable dynamic. Now, simultaneously, in almost every European, Australian and Asian country of the developed world, Smith's other postulate has become praiseworthy, namely, that competition, by setting the acquisitiveness of the one against the acquisitiveness of the others, is a way to discipline capitalism and make it serve the public purpose. Competition, though by definition a state of war, is now a just and necessary war. The social market has become a respected doctrine of the political middle. As in Mandeville's *Fable of the Bees* (1729), it now believes that market competition, that ingenious vice, can raise standards to such heights that the poor live "better than the rich before."

If this were a book of prophecy it would also note a possible transition from a world in which the sovereignty of nations is the foundation of international order, to a world in which the inviolability of persons becomes the foundation of order. A world in which rulers demand non-interference with their right to oppress their own people seems intolerable. But it is far from certain whether, and how, the world will cease to allow such intolerance. It does not matter whether oppression is exercised by a tyrant or by an inequitable social system.

Though of a different category, social harshness, including unemployment, will be opposed if it is seen to have become intrinsic to the economic system – even in a democracy. Business may be pleased that it is a resource of international progress. It may be pleased that it is a resource of work and even dignity. It may be pleased that it is an unsuitable establishment for tyranny. Yet business cannot be pleased if the entrepreneurial efficiency of individual firms results in an aggregate "economics without social efficiency"[6] in a nation.

What is to be done in this age of possimism? (Possimism being the suspicion that good things are possible but won't happen.) The first thing to do is not to expect complete answers, or pretend that there are such. Good may not be a substitute for perfect but it is a sufficient substitute for bad. Collectivity is not as good as individuality, but without a measured proportion of common purpose individualism becomes too quarrelsome.

A short dialogue ensues: **Q:** *Who is the major stakeholder in business as a whole?* **A:** Society. **Q:** *Surely it is the shareholders of the corporation, its employees, the community, the environment, and so on?* **A:** They are the stakeholders in any single corporation; but the chief stakeholder in all corporations is society. **Q:** *What are the purposes of individual corporations?* **A:** Profits, growth, products and services – things like that. **Q:** *Are these compatible with the welfare of society?* **A:** Most of the time. Much of the time. Sometimes. Not always. **Q:** *But is it not enough that business cares about its immediate and near-immediate stakeholders?* **A:** That would certainly be enough in an otherwise rich and just society. Unfortunately, unlike its wealth, the justice of a society is not something business now can do much about. **Q:** *What, then, is to be done?*

Reassert the Ethos of Conviction

What is to be done is to reexamine the meaning of the Ethos of Success, which drives business and its profits; and of the Ethos of Conviction, which drives honor and acceptable behavior. Traditionally, conviction should also drive the "guardians," such as governments, parliaments and civil service samurais. In any case, something more than mere utility must connect the people, the "traders," and the "guardians."

But the Ethos of Success and the Ethos of Conviction are out of phase. Around the turn of the 16th century Francis Bacon spoke of a "conjunction of labours;" there is still a little con-junction now. A false religion is about: many business people adopt such an exclusive religion, which they call "business is business" (whatever that may mean other than an excuse for alternative behavior); while others – citizens, labor, clergy, dip-lomats and armies – suspect that business people are a predatory breed, that business is a separate, incomprehensible establish-ment, and that its institutions are not, in Emerson's words, "the lengthened shadow of a man."

The remedy starts from acceptance that while "private gain remains a necessary condition of commerce it is no longer a sufficient one. The objective now should be not just to make individual companies perform better but also to make the whole system work better."[7] Can business itself helplessly continue to endure the currents and refluxions of a system in which its own interests are repeatedly hurt by recessions, stagnations, unem-ployments and impoverishments, in consequence of which consumption falls, and with it its own continuity, progress, investments, development and research?

Does this imply that businesses should become "political?" Business is not good at politics. Business can band together to voice opinions and offer a view to government, but has no means to implement policies without prejudicing democracy and competition.

Two Cultures: Business and the Other, or the Other, versus the Other

"An adaptive society cannot be controlled by any but adaptive people."[8] The remedy is in the hands of people in business as much as it is in the hands of business as a whole (and probably more). One-hundred and fifty years ago Disraeli warned that there were, in Britain, "two nations; between whom there is no intercourse." Some thirty years ago, C.P. Snow warned against the gulf between science and the arts – he called it the Two Cultures. A similar gulf continues everywhere between the mind of commerce and industry on the one hand, and the mind of non-commercial people – most people – on the other. A grinding noise is often heard when business changes gear to try to talk to people. There is little sense of relatedness between a distant corporation and its folksy commercials.

What is of concern is the unity of civilization. Civilization is the loser whenever an elite – any elite – becomes a severed culture. Things go wrong when a particularist philosophy attempts to dominate – whether it is the leviathan rule of absolute kings; or a Hegelian view of the superior state; or of the military, as in pre-War Japan; or of one party, as in Hitler's Germany; or of one "class," as in Marx's and Lenin's communism. When one part appropriates the whole the chain of shared community is broken.

For plain business people like myself this means that we must not regard people as public markets, or see them merely as consumers of the corporation's outputs.

No need to strain to reacquire virginity. I have noted before[9] that civilization will have its lapses of taste and cannot be entirely pure. There should be room in it for cheerful plainness and lively vulgarity. If it is too tightly swaddled in delicate refinement it loses its refreshment. There is no need for businessmen and women to tread an austere road of virtue, or break their necks from the perpetual exercise of turning the other cheek. But they must not forget the underlying civil purpose of the exercise of business, and must maintain a civilized intention behind the banter, persiflage, and laughter.

A Brief Reflection on Corporate Mor(t)ality

If it is true that corporations are in practice mortal; if they can go into slow decline or suffer sudden death; if they can pass from one owner to another; if they can merge their own identity with another corporation; – then their provisions for share-holders and stakeholders are conditional and contingent. Therefore, stating the obvious, corporations, singly, are dependent systems. They cannot be integral, self-contained social institutions with an irrevocable operating license.

If corporations must adjust the numbers they employ to accord with prevailing technology; if the number they employ is contingent on their financial condition; if the number they employ reduces when they are themselves victims of national or international competition, recessions and depressions; if through thinnings, downsizings and dismissals they decrease corporate risk, but increase social risk thereby; if those they must dismiss become a general charge not on themselves, but on the community or nation; – then, again stating the obvious, they cannot be integral, self-contained social institutions.

If corporations put the interest of their shareholders first (as by law they ultimately must); if they make (immediate or defer-red) profits the measure of success (as in good sense they must); if they therefore abide more by an ethos of measurable successes than by an ethos of unmeasurable moral convic-tions; – then, once more stating the obvious, corporations, singly, are dependent systems, and cannot be integral, self-contained social institutions.

If the nature, work, duty and obligation of the corporation depends on public sentiment, the rule of laws, constitutions and acts of congresses or parliaments; if these treat corpora-tions as partly social institutions which must support the general welfare and other public purpose; – then corporations, singly, cannot be integral, self-contained social institutions. They remain dependent systems.

And so – notwithstanding some elitist fancies – if corporations as a whole depend on the grace, favor and priorities of superior institutions; if the provisions they make for their stakeholders can be altered by the laws of the nation(s) in which they operate and by the civilization(s) they inhabit; if the provisions they make for their stakeholders can be withdrawn or reduced when adversity overwhelms them; – then corporate benevolence is not enough. That is not to say that public-spirited motives and social action are deficiencies. On the contrary: in addition to their commercial purposes corporations *are* partly social institutions; their proper behavior is to the good, and for the good of most. But though these things are not deficiencies they are insufficiencies.

Civilization demands participation not only by corporations as corporations, but by all who work in them. A corporation needs the civility of all participants. Since it is a constituent part of the civilization of its nation, and a part also of the comity of the nations among whom it resides or trades, the corporation must participate with the conviction of its individual members as well as with corporate conviction.

In its entirety, the community of profit-based corporations must not be seen to be a rich, barbaric incubus inside the culture of a nation whose civility is otherwise inclined. It must be seen not to have its own self-indulgent, esoteric culture divorced from the felt experience of the community at large. I do not mean that professions may not have their own cultures of industry. But I mean and deplore a culture of business that inclines to particularism and to an outlook too distant from the general culture; that regards a government which sometimes speaks to interests not its own as perverse; that tends to regard the consumer as its potters' clay.

In business, the limit to virtue is its cost. Any business must, and that quite properly, restrict the amount it spends on the practice of its public benevolence to the limits set by the law and by accepted accountancy criteria. And so, since the will of business is not necessarily the will of a nation, neither business or the market can be a final arbiter of what society chooses to be society's good. Consequently, people in business must share in the civilities and probities of life even before they share in the skills of their profession.

Summary and General Conclusions

There are still other and greater hopes, not derived from within business organizations alone: "They come from schools and from teachers; from universities and philosophers; from men of deep human instincts who are, by occasional miracle, saints. Their strength comes from instincts and impulses deeper perhaps than any of us understand. If these impulses, as we hope they may, continue to demand the self-realization of individuals, if they continue to call for methods, institutions and remedies making it possible for every man to protect his personality against invasion, then society emerging in the capitalist revolution will continue to be free."

Adolf A. Berle, *The 20th Century Capitalist Revolution*,
Harcourt Brace, New York, 1954

Prognostication is foolhardy. It is better to state known trends and make moderate suggestions. Some trends are these:

Industrial societies, capitalism, and business as a dominant economic force, have grown immeasurably for over a century. Yet their discontinuity with the rest of society continues. Partial economic theories of capitalist mechanisms abound and partial sociologies of society over-abound; but a convincing theory of capitalism *and* society is absent. It may be that such a theory is impossible because society is a moving target, and shifting technology and capitalism an even faster-moving target.

It may also be that an integrating economic and social theory is not desirable. The last time a comprehensive theory was given a long run – by Marx, Engels, Lenin, and Stalin – it showed up the poverty of "scientific" philosophy and ended in malice, blood, police and inanition. We know that democracy is messy, that pluralism is messy, that "free" enterprise is messy – and that their histories and logic, as described, are messier still. But we also know that these mixed stews are in large part the outcome of compromises that Western nations have made and of tolerances they have shown. The West is now inclined to forgo the elegance of logical coherence in favor of reasonable hopes of progress and forbearance.

The concept of a Western capitalism run by "capitalists" is long gone. There are now many millions of individuals and families who have adequate capital earned and saved. To these, capital is a classical repository or store of wealth. Their financial investments are a means of net worth maintenance – or better. The problems they have with the husbandry of their wealth, with risk, of their dealings with internal revenue services, and of their need of advisors, lawyers and accountants, are not very different from the problems of corporate housekeeping. The difference between them is that corporations are molders of capitalism and individuals are users of it.

The notion of consumers as a class is new. More or less collective-minded economies, even those of humanitarian benevolence such as Germany's, Japan's or Switzerland's, whose laws were more protective of industrial and mercantile interests than those of the general public, are beginning to rescind unbalanced legislation of the past. But what is a useful categorization for marketing purposes is, socially, a single-sided portraiture. The division into man-as-producer and man-as-consumer is a piece of unacceptable scission. If capitalism is to continue its successes it must reconcile this unbalancing dualism. It is absurd to have one and the same person made happy as consumer but unhappy as producer (and *vice versa*). Can producers who put their money into a pension scheme for their own consumption in old age be classified as either?

Little that has not been said elsewhere need here be said of environment and demography. Food and health for growing populations will be an undoubted problem for the world, but probably no major problem for the West, and probably not for Japan and the prosperous shores of Asia.[10] A more immediate problem for them is the growth of wealth and the growing propinquity of neighbors. In one Swiss hamlet, though the number of villagers rose little, this writer saw a near-doubling of the number of houses is less than a decade. Building had become a function not of population but of rising wealth and rich divorces. It brought fulfillable demands for ampler private space with them. But with growing incursions on public spaces, and with increasing density, new laws will come to buffer conflicts which arise from noisy assertions of the rights of property and the impingement of neighbors on each other (including corporate neighbors). Whether one likes it or not, legislatures and laws will speak more loudly and more often. Hopes of minimal governance by a "minimum state" are unlikely to be met. As for industry and corporations, they will have to choose between helping to draft good laws or to be drafted by them. It is however certain that an increasing density of populations or of wealth will require more social responsibility. A proportionately large amount of it will have to be borne by business.

Wealth is diffusing from developed to other countries. Some, many, in the West complain of "giant sucking noises" from poorer countries, which they believe diminish their own jobs and incomes. Sixty or so years ago, the economists R.F. Kahn and J.M. Keynes postulated a "multiplier" mechanism by which (very roughly) every dollar spent on investment in an economy becomes income for others and generates secondary, tertiary, and so on incomes. Successive total yields from this diffusion may be low (say 0.5) or it may be considerable (say 10). Keynes presciently said that

"In an open system with foreign-trade relations, some part of the multiplier of the increased investment will accrue to the benefit of employment in foreign countries..." "On the other hand, our own country may recover a portion of this leakage through favourable repercussions due to the action of the multiplier in the foreign country in increasing its economic activity."[11]

That is what happened and is happening now. Part (but only part) of the multiplier has leaked abroad. Soon the leak leaks back and yields dividends. Countries with low labor costs prosper and turn into countries with higher labor costs, higher standards of living and increased purchasing power. They soon become customers of the source country. Germany and France are early post-War examples; Japan and Singapore are late post-War examples. Free trade and open markets make wealth and will continue to do so unless false argument prevails.

I turn to this book's main concern: the disparity of the mind of business from the mind of the rest of society. Of this A.N. Whitehead said, as long ago as 1933, that

"[T]he motive of success is not enough. It produces a short-sighted world which destroys the sources of its own prosperity. [W]e must not fall into the fallacy of thinking of the business world in abstraction from the rest of the community. The behaviour of the community is largely dominated by the business mind."[12]

The problem is not new and we have lived with it for many years. It has no clear and present urgency. Why raise it now?

It will matter because, if "the behavior of the community is largely dominated by the business mind," then whether it is a good and acceptable mind will be a subject of continuous debate.

It will matter because of the growth of wealth and the impingement of many neighbors on each other; because of the increasing density of populations and the businesses that serve and supply them; and because of the increasing complexities of life.

It will matter because businesses are the prime carrier of economic achievement – and so are people who work in them as co-producers and consumers.

It will matter because the expansion of humanitarianism and the welfare state has left humanism with few established patrons other than business as a natural and proper locus and payer-in-part. Business has created private wealth for many and has thereby to some degree enhanced the dignity of life. It must now turn to conditions for non-material enrichment.

What is advocated is both corporate and individual; generational and gradual; important rather than urgent; not for immediate programs but for addenda to a corporation's business purposes; a change of set of mind, disposition or mentality; an awareness of the social consequences of corporate activity; above all, a recognition that reasonableness is not concession, and that concession is not defeat.

Civilization is not peculiar to a corporation but surrounds it. No corporate policy can be wrong that encourages its members to regard the public interest as part of its own; that encourages them to be "social entrepreneurs" and spend time in community activities, charities and the arts, at home and abroad; that asks them to see their own work as though through a public eye; that allows that business minds can be efficient and generous with or without a profit motive; and that assists government to be a better guardian of the common interest. There are signs that this is beginning to happen, but not yet widely as corporate stance and policy. It will take time.

Business must not be a disparate elite. The general question is about corporate additions to the diffusion of civility. Although corporations alone cannot directly raise the measure of required civility in the education of the young, they can pursue an ambience of civility within to all who work in them, and thereby spill it over to the generations.

Earlier chapters spoke of the Ethos of Success and of the Ethos of Conviction. They said that all the virtues – faith, hope, charity, justice, fortitude – are bunched inside the Ethos of Conviction, but that all the great rewards of this world – power and wealth – abide in the Ethos of Success. It is entirely possible to volunteer some wealth and power to participation and civility.

Coda

A conversation between Richard Koch (RK) and the author (IA), December 1996.

RK: If I am an executive who wants to be fully "industrious and civilized," how should I change my daily behavior at work? What, specifically, do you want me to stop or start doing? And what should corporations themselves be doing differently?

IA: I deliberately make no programmatic suggestions. I am talking about changes over the next ten or twenty years, about a generational shift in paradigms – in the mentality of business. What matters is a change of attitude and internal ambience.

What should individuals do and not do? At heart, what is important is what they should *not* do: think and act as if they belonged to a separate world. Not only is this arrogant, but it is also against the tenets of good business: you cannot regard the "consumer" as both valued master and untutored quarry. One reason why the problem arises is that, while public democracies are not command structures, private corporations mostly are. As a result, an alienating, autocratic turn of mind too often prevails in them.

Being "civilized" as an individual is a state of mind, a systematic spirit of enquiry, aims and values – rather than a program of deeds. It will find its own actions, if the corporate ambience also changes.

It is easier to give some specific examples of what civilized corporations should do, because there are promising signs already. According to the US Conference Board, "social service leave" and other (mostly) paid sabbaticals have been introduced by many American companies: Xerox, American Express and perhaps about one-hundred other Fortune 500 corporations. And in Europe lately, the *Centre des Jeunes Dirigeants d'Entreprise*, the French "Centre of Young CEOs," published a sweeping 150-page report which maintains that companies should be judged on their contribution to the well-being of society. British Aerospace, a corporation with over 40,000 staff, is to establish a "virtual university" for its engineers and grant them study leave – something that Motorola and other US and a few British and European corporations are already doing. So the change of mentality is beginning to diffuse.

RK: If I spend some paid time helping to educate society about business or providing some other service to the community for which the firm is not compensated, won't I make it less competitive and less able to service society in the focused way it should? What right have I as a manager to decide to allocate resources to something that is not directly in the interest of customers or shareholders? And doesn't experience suggest that when managers arbitrate between the claims of different stakeholders, all that happens is that management itself becomes larger, more powerful and more self-serving? Like government, doesn't management tend to pervert "the public good" by expanding what it does, ending up by providing poor value for money simply because it is not focused on narrow commercial objectives?

IA: The definition of "narrow commercial objectives" and of "what is not *directly* in the interest of customers or shareholders" is an old problem and could equally well call into question all sorts of things that *are* accepted: the redecoration of a CEO's office, the provision of pensions and brighter lavatories, the propriety of charitable or cultural grants, party-political contributions, founding libraries, and so on. For example, Microsoft's grounds are like a large, well-groomed park. Companies do many things which are not narrowly cost-effective, but which make sense from a broader or more long-term point of view. Cheeseparing is hardly the way to real progress.

In truth, managements are already the arbiters. Who else can be? The question is whether they are wise arbiters. As to power, by all means let managements be powerful – for nothing is worse than weak, smug and indecisive managements – as long as they are responsible and not stubbornly self-serving.

The true criterion is whether a corporate action is good for the corporation as a going concern and whether it conforms with acceptable standards of behavior. In this, the corporate *persona* differs in few ways from the actions of individuals.

RK: What, in your view, is likely to happen if corporations and executives do not become more "industrious and civilized?" Do you really think that society will reject the business system that enriches it? Isn't it difficult to see an alternative system gaining ground now that communism is three-quarters dead and socialism is in retreat?

IA: For all practical purposes, communism is wholly dead. I am assured by knowledgeable friends that it is difficult, even in China, to find a believing Marxist. But "social"-ism – as public and political humanitarianism – is in full bloom in most Western nations, even those under the aegis of otherwise temperately conservative governments. It may have to retreat a little because it has overspent (in Scandinavia, Germany, France and Italy, for example) but it will remain.

What will happen if corporations and executives do not become more "industrious and civilized?" Who can tell? St Augustine somewhere says that time only speaks in syllables. Like you, I can see no radically alternative orchestrations to replace the business system. But government, while it may try to slim, will not shrink in sovereign and supervisory powers. Nor will it lose its tendency to play to the electorate. It therefore depends on business itself. It will retain integrity as a valued institution if it manages to be one – against increasingly high standards. If not, it will be curbed and checked.

RK: You say that we are at the end of the Age of Reason. What age will we enter in the next century?
IA: We have not had an Age of Reason. We have had attempts at it, ending with the collapse of Soviet communism. As to the next age, though I am not sure, we may have reached a watershed.

The last two centuries or so, as we have seen in previous pages, have been a time in which belief in progress and in "human reason" elicited many attempts to define the Ends of Man and the nature of the Good Society.

The United States through its Constitution, and to an extent France, continued with many Enlightenment ideas. There also arose in the 19th century continental Europe a rising consciousness of nationhood and of the state as its public guardian. But because the state often turned out to be more an oppressor than a guardian, Marx invented a universal revolutionary victory by the common man. This bet on reason failed wretchedly.

What is left? No utopian public philosophy. Little belief in the inevitability of progress. Even less belief in the infinite perfectibility of man. And a lot of doubt about even the possibility of a *science* of society. No one proposes a new Age of Reason. Instead, one discerns a mood of what may whimsically be called possimism: a conviction that good things are possible but will not happen unless we try very hard indeed – and must therefore strive to be both industrious *and* civilized. We have just enough belief in reasonableness to make a future Age of Accommodation possible. Business can play a major part in this, because, though few are aware of it, the most useful and successful tools of business have always been accommodation, tolerance and compromise.

RK: You talk a lot about the "culture of business" but isn't what you really mean "the American business culture?" You stress the national differences in the evolution of capitalism, but is there a serious, effective and distinctive business culture today that is not essentially American? Is Japanese business culture really different? French? German? To the extent that other business cultures are different, are they not inherently less progressive, egalitarian and meritocratic?

IA: You are in essence asking whether Samuel Huntington's celebrated *Clash of Civilizations* (*Fortune*, Summer 1993) also applies to business: "[I]n the former Soviet Union, communists can become democrats, the rich can become poor and the poor rich, but Russians cannot become Estonians and Azeris cannot become Armenians," and, by implication, that *national* characteristics overarch such international phenomena as business. Or whether the Japanese observer Masakazu Yamazaki is more correct (*Asia, a Civilization in the Making, Fortune*, 1996): he believes that *Western world civilization* overarches distinct national civilizations. So, I see, does Mrs Kumaratunga, the President of Sri Lanka, who, in reply to a question as to whether "Western" values may be challenged by "Asian" values, says that the free market has become universal and that "[w]hen people talk about a conflict of values, I think it is an excuse that can be used to cover a multitude of sins" (*International Herald Tribune*, November 29, 1996).

We may safely conclude that industrialism and capitalism have become universal mechanisms. Though America still provides an admirable dynamic, capitalism is not exclusively American. And yes, European business is still more inclined than American to "arranged" markets.

So is Japanese business. The Japanese system was, in the first half of this century, given to as much conflict and exploitation of labor as were Britain and the USA, until a "samurai" system and code of honor was adapted for business and deliberately introduced. This is the difference between Japan and the

West: the latter's business system has civilian origins, whereas Japan adopted a system of quasi-feudal reciprocal duty of servant to master and master to servant. The distinction is beginning to weaken but will continue for many years. The West has moved "from status to contract;" but in Japan, still, status *is* contract. The Japanese method has, as we know, great drawbacks but some merits. It blends the ethic of success with the ethic of conviction more smoothly than the West.

Still, we are talking about nuances, not essences. Capitalism has become universal and international. Take German banking: German industrialists are beginning to escape from German banks, while German banks are coming to London to participate in international banking. Circles.

In the end, we can't have two or more capitalisms. The logic of money prevails. "Quality" is forcing up standards. Applied transnational technology diffuses good practice and is a long-term antidote to nationalism. So I do not believe in particularist European or Asian capitalisms which are said to be more "civilized" than American capitalism. All business should conform to conscionable standards of civility.

RK: Isn't the word "civilized," as applied by you to business culture and executives, a trappy and ambiguous concept? "Civilized" may mean more humanistic, cultured, sophisticated, educated and elitist. Yet "civilized" can also mean decent, egalitarian, humanitarian, caring and considerate? You seem to mean both senses. But don't they run in different directions? Aren't you confusing things – or which sense do you really mean?

IA: It's not that complicated. Civilization is the way of life, the manners, mores, habits, attitudes, taboos and values which prevail in a community, and which increase the understanding of our fellows. Civilization is the basic, often unspoken and implicit, mode of communication. Culture, on the other hand, is the architecture of innovation, science, art, writing, and "cultural" activities, which builds on civilization and enriches it, renews it, or changes it.

What concerns me is the dualism between the present ideals of civility of society and the harder-edged civility one often observes in the world of business. The latter's values – at times an almost complete reliance on the calculus and ethic of success – are in danger of becoming divorced from the ethic of conviction shared by both ordinary people and leaders outside the world of business. It won't do – it just won't work – to carry this disparity forward into the more interdependent and ever denser world of the future. I'm not saying that the problem is acute and that we are at a point of crisis, but the problem grows and should be recognized. Humanism implies learning and humanitarianism implies caring. Both have their place.

RK: So you say that business should have an extended humanitarian role – for example, that it should take on some welfare functions?
IA: Put like that, no. Not beyond what propriety requires. But I do believe that business can and should have a *humanist* role.

RK: You say that business must not be a separate elite, but isn't this inevitable and even desirable? Aren't elites always separate, whether they be the government elite, or the show-biz elite, or the academic elite?
IA: Well, we can both agree that business should not be more divorced from society than any other institution – say government. Now, one form of government or another has been with us throughout all history. We have found ways of taming and civilizing government. But where are the constitutions, parliaments and congresses of business? Its regulators are, first, competition; next, positive legislation; last, public morality. Yes, these have worked fairly well. But all of them are extrinsic forces. Business needs more than this; it needs something intrinsic and internal: the sort of constitutional spirit found in good parliaments and congresses. An institution such as business –

powerful in the aggregate, a shaper of civilization, universal –
ought to acquire an intrinsic, internally bred public philosophy.

As to elites, like the poor, they will ever be with us. Most of
them are play groups. Some even do some good. Good black-
smiths are an elite; so are jewelers, and business people from all
the various branches of industry and services. They are elites
because they have a common source of professional pride. A
harmful elite is one which is impermeable and based on power.

*RK: I am worried that you imply that corporations have a social
responsibility in maintaining employment. Isn't this romantic Lud-
ditism? Jack Welch of General Electric insists that "only the customer
can guarantee employment." Isn't he right? And what's wrong with
letting unemployment sort itself out as a result of economic growth? Do
you think that the unerring medium and long-term link between
increased efficiency and increased employment – a link that has been
evident since at least the 17th century – has suddenly and permanently
snapped?*

IA: What concerns me is that, while corporations have the right
to fire, the unemployed are sustained from tax revenues, i.e. by
taxpayers. Individual citizens have to pay for problems they
have not caused. That is an anomaly.

*RK: You might as well say that business created employment in the first
place, but has not been rewarded for this. Perhaps this is all semantics.
The real question I want to ask is this: do you have any remedies for
unemployment?*

IA: Economists appear to have few satisfactory answers, and
businesses can walk away from the problem because sustaining
the unemployed is not their responsibility.

One tentative remedy – one that must undergo severely
critical examination – may be a removal of corporation-tax revenues from government budgets (wholly or in large part) to a
ring-fenced all-corporations fiduciary fund – privatized and

properly funded. Corporations would then become collectively responsible for legally defined and scaled unemployment compensation, as well as for training, retraining, apprenticeships, and so forth (excluding pensions). All corporations would continue to have the right to hire and fire, but would have good reason to be increasingly careful and conscientious.

The addition of such custodial duties to the corporate system would give real institutional meaning to "stakeholding" and a "stakeholder society" – concepts which sound wonderful, but are too vague and insubstantial.

But I want to answer your earlier question: No, I do not think that corporations have a social responsibility in maintaining employment. What I do say is that corporations have a social responsibility. Not quite the same thing. And, ultimately, business cannot love someone as consumer and sack him or her as producer. I don't want to make an absurd reduction of this argument, but were a high proportion of the working population to be made jobless – in the interests of lower prices – how many would remain effective consumers even if goods were cheaper or better? You could then turn round Jack Welch's aphorism and say that only employment can guarantee customers. It is in the interests of business itself to join in finding solutions to this problem, and not say it is none of its concern. The business system had best remain a wealth-making, not a misery-making system.

Yes, there was full employment in the Middle Ages. It was scratching to keep the wolf from the door. We can do better than that.

RK: *Are you an optimist? Are you a closet believer in Progress? Do you acquiesce in Edward Gibbon's "pleasing conclusion that every age of the world has increased, and still increases, the real wealth, the happiness, the knowledge, and perhaps the virtue, of the human race?"*
IA: All of us in this business are itsy pragmatists, bitsy idealists,

and itsy-bitsy millenarians who believe in the *possibility* of progress. Gibbon's dictum is not the truth but an ideal.

RK: If you had to sum up your whole message in one sentence, what would it be?
IA: Conventional. As in John Donne's Devotions: "every man is a piece of the continent, a part of the main" – which includes corporations and executives.

Notes and References

Chapter 1

1. Isaiah Berlin, *Russian Thinkers – Herzen and Bakunin on Liberty*, Viking, New York, 1978, p. 98. Berlin quoting Herzen's "From the Other Shore," VI 110.
2. James Burnham, *The Managerial Revolution*, John Day Co., New York, 1941 pp. 224–6.
3. This mention gratefully draws on Haynes Johnson, *International Herald Tribune/Washington Post*, January 29, 1992.
4. Evsey D. Domar, "How I Tried to Become an Economist," in *Eminent Economists*, ed. M. Szenberg, Cambridge University Press, Cambridge and New York, 1992, p. 117.
5. W.W. Rostow, "Reflections on Political Economy," in *Eminent Economists*, ed. M. Szenberg, Cambridge University Press, Cambridge and New York, 1992, p. 229.
6. Thorstein Veblen, *The Theory of Business Enterprise*, Scribner, New York, 1904/1936, pp. 309, 295.
7. Graham Wallas, *The Great Society*, Macmillan, New York, 1914/1936, pp. 309, 295.
8. J.A. Schumpeter, "The March into Socialism," address to the American Economic Association in New York in 1949, in *Capitalism, Socialism and Democracy*, Harper & Row, New York, 3rd edition 1947/1950, pp. 417, 419. Later writers, among them Robert L. Heilbronner in his *Business Civilization in Decline*,

Norton, New York, 1976, have echoed and amplified Schumpeter's thesis.

9. Quoted in Leopold Schwarzschild, *World in Trance*, Hamish Hamilton, London, 1943, p. 126.
10. Walther Rathenau, *Die Neue Wirtschaft*, S. Fischer, Berlin, 1918, pp. 36/7, 73. Present author's translation.
11, 12. Walter Rathenau, *Von Kommenden Dingen* (1916) Trans.: *In Days to Come*, Allen & Unwin, London, 1921, pp. 123, 50, 75, 26.
13. *Ford on Management*, Intro. R. Lessem, Blackwell, Oxford, 1991, pp. 10, 141, 148 (Reissue of Henry Ford's *My Life and Work*, 1922, and *My Philosophy of Industry*, 1929).
14. M.L. Severy, *Gillette's Social Redemption*, Chatto & Windus, London, 1907, p. 737.
15. King C[amp] Gillette, *World Corporation*, New England News Co., 1910, pp. 4, 7, 42, 43, 71, 103, 105, 119, 121, 151, 199.
16. Jacques Bolle, "Solvay 1863-1963", Weissenbruch, Brussels, pp. 178/9. Present author's translation.
17. "A Documentary History of Communism," University Press of New England, 1984, Hanover NH and London. From the editor's, R.V. Daniels's introduction, the *New Economic Policy*.
18. V.I. Lenin, April 1921, "The Tax In Kind," ibid., p. 144, on *NEP*, the *New Economic Policy*.

Chapter 2

1. J.B. Bury, *The Idea of Progress*, Macmillan, New York, 1932, p. 5.
2. Robert Nisbet, *History of the Idea of Progress*, Basic Books, New York, 1980, p. 357.
3. G.K. Chesterton, *Orthodoxy*, John Lane, London & New York, 1909, pp. 50/1.
4. Boris Yeltsin, *Against the Grain*, Jonathan Cape, London, 1990, p. 113.

5. Oskar Morgenstern and John von Neumann, *The Theory of Games and Economic Behaviour*, 3rd ed., University Press Princeton, 1953.

6. Oskar Morgenstern, "Game Theory," in *Dictionary of the History of Ideas*, Scribner, New York, 1968, 1973, vol. II, p. 274.

7. Isaiah Berlin, *The Crooked Timber of Humanity* (*The Decline of Utopian Ideas in the West*), John Murray, London, 1990, p. 48.

8. Charles Darwin, *The Origin of Species*, London, 1859, ch. XIV, p. 489.

9. This paragraph draws on Alan E. Bernstein, *Hell: Death and Retribution in the Ancient and Early Christian Worlds*, UCL Press, London, 1993, pp. 55/6.

10. Adam Smith, *The Theory of Moral Sentiments*, 1759, and *The Wealth of Nations*, 1776. Adam Smith was not the first to say this. In the middle of the 16th century, two hundred years before Smith, Hale wrote his *Discourse on Usury*, in which the following words occur: "... that [which] is proffitable to one, so to a nother, maie be proffitable to all, and so to the common wealth."

11. Adolf Berle and Gardiner Means, *The Modern Corporation*, Macmillan, New York, 1933.

12. Alfred D. Chandler Jr., *The Visible Hand*, Belknap Press, Cambridge, MA, 1977.

13. Julian Huxley, *New Bottles for New Wine*, Chatto & Windus, London, 1957, p. 34.

14. The physicist Roger Penrose has used a similar argument about the human brain. He used it to cast doubt on whether human and computer minds are comparable.

15. Stephen Hawking, *A Brief History of Time*, Bantam Press, London, 1988.

16. Stephen Weinberg, *The First Three Minutes*, Basic Books, New York, 1977.

17. John Passmore, *The Perfectibility of Man*, Duckworth, London, 1970, pp. 326/7.

Chapter 3

1. Reinold Noyes, *The Institution of Property in Anglo-American Law*, Longman Green & Co., New York and Toronto, 1936, pp. 267, 431.
2. *Encyclopaedia of Social Sciences*, "Property," 1937.
3. John R. Commons, *Legal Foundations of Capitalism*, Macmillan Co., New York, 1924, p. 52.
4. Ivan Alexander, *Foundations of Business*, Basil Blackwell, Oxford, and Cambridge, Massachusetts, 1990, pp. 180/1.
5. The Massachusetts Bill of Rights, written by John Adams – one example among many.

   I do not here argue the difference between ownership or seisin, possession, and custody. The subject is beyond the scope of this book.
6. Pope Leo XIII's 1891 encyclical, *"Rerum Novarum."*
7. Pope John Paul II's 1991 encyclical, *"Centesimus Annus."*
8. Jacques Ellul, "Theological Foundations of Law" (1946), SCM Press, London, 1961.

   For brevity, I do not draw a distinction in this chapter between divine and "self-evident" natural law. Ellul argues that natural law does not exist apart from divine ordinance. It can be argued that "divine command as natural law" is contradictory. The argument would run like this: An omnipotent God is able to create any kind of world and many kinds of worlds. In choosing to create the world we know, He was like a painter who painted what he chose to paint. Thus nature is His work of art. And if it is a work of art, then there are no natural laws – only His design. If so, such laws are not natural laws but positive, deliberate laws.

   If, on the contrary, anyone does not believe that God is the Creator, then "natural" has no authority or relevance, because no norms follow from things that are as they are.
9. Hegel's *Philosophy of Right*, trans. T.M. Knox, Oxford

University Press, Oxford, 1945/1953, para. 272, p. 285. Hegel's wording was *irdisch-göttlich.*

10. Dean Roscoe Pound, *An Introduction to the Philosophy of Law,* 1922, revised edition, Yale University Press, New Haven, 1954, p. 132.

Chapter 4

1. Isaiah Berlin, *The Crooked Timber of Humanity,* John Murray, London, 1990, p. 180.

2. Joseph de Maistre, 1753–1821, *Soirées de Saint-Pétersbourg.*

3. Ivan Alexander, *Foundations of Business,* Basil Blackwell, Oxford and Cambridge, Massachusetts, 1990, p. 43. "A passion for equality..." quotes Lord Acton.

4. Robert Nozick, *The Nature of Rationality,* Princeton University Press, Princeton, NJ, 1993, p. 181. The full sentence reads: "Our principles fix what our life stands for, our aims create the light our life is bathed in, and our rationality, both individual and coordinate, defines and symbolizes the distance we have come from mere animality."

5. John Rawls, *Political Liberalism,* Columbia University Press, New York, 1993.

Chapter 5

1. John P. Davis, *Corporations,* Capricorn Books, NY, 1961 (1897), vol. 2, p. 2.

2. Ernst Troeltsch, "The Ideas of Natural Law and Humanity in World Politics," 1922. Lecture included as Appendix 1 in Otto Gierke, *Natural Law and the Theory of Society 1500–1800.* Ed., intro. & trans. Ernest Barker, Cambridge University Press, 1934, pp. 202/204.

3. Ernst Troeltsch, lecture on "The Historical School of Law,"

quoted by Ernest Barker in his introduction to Gierke's *Natural Law and the Theory of Society*, p. liv.

4. Elie Kedourie, *Nationalism*, Hutchinson, London, 1960. 4th expanded edition, Blackwell Publishers, Oxford & Cambridge, MA, 1993, p. xvi, ch. 6, ch. 7.

5. Jane Jacobs, *Systems of Survival, a Dialogue on the Moral Foundations of Commerce and Policies*, Random House, New York, 1991; Hodder & Stoughton, London, 1993.

Chapter 6

1. Adolf Berle, *The Twentieth Century Capitalist Revolution*, 1955.
2. E. Lipson, *Economic History of England*, A&C Black, London, 6th ed., 1956, vol. II, p. 269.
3. E. Lipson, *Economic History of England*, A&C Black, London, 6th ed., 1956, vol. II, p. 314.
4. John P. Davis, *Corporations*, Capricorn Books, NY, 1961 (1897), v. 2, pp. 242, 246, 280.
5. Henry Sumner Maine, *Ancient Law*, 10th ed., 1906, p. 200.
6. Edward S. Mason, ed., *The Corporation in Modern Society*, Harvard University Press, Cambridge, MA, 1959, pp. 1/2.
7. Gardiner C. Means, "Capitalism and Economic Theory," in *The Corporation Take-over*, Harper & Row, New York, 1964, p. 83.
8. Richard Eells and Clarence Walton, *Conceptual Foundations of Business*, Richard Irwin Inc., Homewood, ILL, 1961, p. 514.
9. John P. Davis, *Corporations*, Capricorn Books, NY, 1961 (1897), footnote v. 1, p. 5.
10. A.P. Smith Manufacturing Company v. Barlow et al., 98 A2[d] 581.

Chapter 7

1. Foreword by Robert Merton to Jacques Ellul's *The Technological Society*, Random House, New York, revised American edition, 1964.

2. Robert M. Hutchins, *Two Faces of Federalism*, Center for the Study of Democratic Institutions, Santa Barbara, California, 1961, p. 22.
3. Robert Bridges, *The Testament of Beauty*, London, 1929.
4. J.M. Keynes, "The End of Laissez-faire," 1926, included in *Essays in Persuasion*, London, 1931, pp. 314/5.
5. Adolf A. Berle Jr. and Gardiner C. Means, *The Modern Corporation and Private Property*, Macmillan, New York, 1932.
6. Alfred D. Chandler, *The Visible Hand*, The Belknap Press of Harvard University Press, Cambridge, MA, 1977.
7. Andrew Shonfield, *Modern Capitalism*, Royal Institute of International Affairs and Oxford University Press, London, 1965, pp. 246–264.

Chapter 8

1. Peter F. Drucker, *The New Realities*, Harper & Row, New York, 1989, p. 180.
2. Joseph A. Schumpeter, *Capitalism, Socialism and Democracy*, Harper, New York, 1942.
3. Robert L. Heilbronner, *Business Civilization in Decline*, Norton, New York, 1976.
4. Adolf A. Berle Jr., *Power Without Property*, Sidgwick & Jackson, London, 1960, p. 27.
5. Adam Smith, *The Wealth of Nations*, 5th ed., 1789, reprinted Chicago University Press, 1976, vol. 2, bk. V., ch. 1, p. 264.
6. Adolf A. Berle Jr. and Gardiner C. Means, *The Modern Corporation and Private Property*, Macmillan, New York, 1932, p. 277.
7. Irving S. Shapiro, with C.B. Kaufmann, *America's Third Revolution, Public Interest and the Private Role*, Harper & Row, New York, 1984, pp. ix/x.
8. Adolf A. Berle Jr. and Gardiner C. Means, *The Modern Corporation and Private Property*, Macmillan, New York, 1932, p. 221.

9. *The Corporation Take-Over*, ed. Andrew Hacker, Harper & Row, New York, 1964. Introduction by Andrew Hacker, p. 13.

Chapter 9

1. J.M. Keynes, *The General Theory of Employment, Interest and Money*, Macmillan, London, 1947, p. 374.
2. Charles Darwin, *Voyage of the Beagle*, 1839, chapter on "Slavery."
3. J.M. Keynes, *The General Theory of Employment, Interest and Money*, Macmillan, London, 1947, p. 379.
4. A distinction is to be drawn between individual "rationality" and the "rationality" of the market as a whole.

   As long ago as 1936, J.M. Keynes (in *The General Theory*, Macmillan, London, p. 155) noted that while the social object of skilled investment should be to "defeat the dark forces of time and ignorance which envelop our future," the actual, private object of the most skilled investment in his day was to " 'beat the gun' " and "outwit the crowd." Such is still the case sixty years later – whether the guesswork is called "street smarts," or "rational expectations," or "adaptive expectations." Some economists, notably George Akerlof in California and Frank Hahn in Britain, have tried to examine the effects of "near-rationality" with the aid of related sociologies.

   But this does not help to answer the following important questions: Can rationality at one level result in irrationality at another level? Is the sum of many rational individual decisions necessarily rational? Is the outcome rational after the market has smeared out faulty individual decisions? In other words, is The Market rational *as a whole*?

   To that, there are two answers. One often-given answer is, Yes, the market is always right. This, however, amounts to no more than an assertion that "that that is, is;" or, extended, "that that is, is right." Unfortunately, the corollary of this extended assertion is that "that that was, was right." The proposition is thus a piece of circular reasoning, and meaningless.

The second answer is, unsurprisingly, that we have not yet found complete answers. And so, if it turns out (as seems likely) that the answers lie within Game Theory (see Chapter 2), we shall have to forgo perfection and settle for optimizing policies – a not unreasonable outcome.

5. Fernand Braudel, *Grammaire de civilisations*, 1987. Trans. Richard Mayne as *A History of Civilizations*, Allan Lane, London and New York, 1994, p. 168.

6. W.W. Rostow, "Reflections on Political Economy," in *Eminent Economists*, ed. M. Szenberg, Cambridge University Press, Cambridge and New York, 1992, p. 226.

7. Kenneth J. Arrow, "I Know a Hawk from a Handsaw," in *Eminent Economists*, ed. M. Szenberg, Cambridge University Press, Cambridge and New York, 1992, pp. 46/7.

8. Jacques-Bènigne Bossuet, *VIe Avertissements aux protestants*, III, ix, 1689–91.

9. Elisabeth Labrousse, "Toleration," in *Dictionary of the History of Ideas*, Scribner, New York, 1973, vol. IV, pp. 112/3/4/7.

10. Maurice Cranston, *Encyclopaedia of Philosophy*, Macmillan, New York and London, 1967, vol. 8, p. 143.

Chapter 10

1. Anthony Sampson, *The Seven Sisters*, Viking, 1975, pp. 71–9, 7. The better account. I have however used Berle's for its fifties flavor and its ambivalence.

2. Adolf A. Berle, *The Twentieth Century Capitalist Revolution*. Macmillan, London, 1955, pp. 116/127.

3. *Ford on Management*, Intro. R. Lessem, Basil Blackwell, Oxford, 1991 (reprint of Henry Ford's *My Life and Work*, 1922, and *My Philosophy of Industry*, 1929), p. 9.

Chapter 11

1. John Rawls, *A Theory of Justice*, Clarendon Press, Oxford, 1972, p. 291.
2. Charles Darwin, *Voyage of the Beagle*, 1839, chapter on "Slavery."
3. Quoted by Michael Oakeshott in *Morality and Politics in Modern Europe*, Yale University Press, New Haven and London, 1993, p. 66.
4. T.S. Eliot, *The Hollow Men*, 1925.
5. T.V. Houser, Chairman Sears Roebuck, *Big Business and Human Values*, 1957. J.F. Oates, Chairman Equitable Life, *Business and Social Change*, 1968. C.H. Greenewalt, Chairman DuPont, *The Uncommon Man*, 1959. Published by McGraw-Hill, New York (McKinsey Foundation Lectures).
6. The phrase is William Pfaff's, *International Herald Tribune*, early November 1993.
7. I.S. Shapiro, *America's Third Revolution – Public Interest and the Private Role*, Harper & Row, New York, 1984. I.S. Shapiro was chairman of DuPont from 1974 to 1981.
8. Elton Mayo, *The Social Problems of an Industrial Civilization*, Harvard University School of Business Administration, Boston, 1945, p. xi.
9. Ivan Alexander, *Foundations of Business*, Basil Blackwell, Oxford and Cambridge, MA, 1990, pp. 177, 189.
10. At some point, molecular engineering and artificial photosynthesis may invent and produce foods on an industrial scale in factories. The world's problem would then not be hunger but the displacement of millions of smallholders in many poor countries – with major consequences for social stability.
11. J.M. Keynes, *The General Theory of Employment Interest and Money*, Macmillan & Co., London, 1936, p. 120.
12. Alfred North Whitehead, *Adventures of Ideas*, Cambridge University Press, 1933.

Index

Note: 'n.' after a page number indicates the number of a note on that page.